BEYOND STORIES:

YOUNG CHILDREN'S
NONFICTION
COMPOSITION

Susan J. Britsch

EYE ON EDUCATION
6 DEPOT WAY WEST, SUITE 106
LARCHMONT, NY 10538
(914) 833-0551
(914) 833-0761 FAX
www.eyeoneducation.com

For information about permission to reproduce selections from
this book, write: Eye On Education, Permission Dept., Suite 106,
6 Depot Way West, Larchmont, NY 10538

Library of Congress Cataloging-in-Publication Data

Britsch, Susan J., 1955–
    Beyond stories : young children's nonfiction composition
  / Susan J. Britsch.
        p. cm.
    Includes bibliographical references.
    ISBN 1-930556-40-3
        1. English language—Composition and exercises—Study
and teaching (Early childhood)   2. English language—
Composition and exercises—Study and teaching (Primary)
3. Exposition (Rhetoric)   I. Title: Young children's
nonfiction composition.   II. Title.

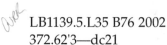 LB1139.5.L35 B76 2002
    372.62'3—dc21

                                            2002019383

Those who are really innovative and really
powerful are those who break conventions,
not those who reproduce them.

Cope and Kalantzis, 1993

Table of Contents

About the Author

Susan J. Britsch is associate professor of Literacy and Language Education in the Department of Curriculum and Instruction at Purdue University. A former preschool teacher, her interests include the development of children's original storytelling, children's writing in nonfiction genres, and the integration of science and literacy curricula in elementary schools. She has published numerous academic articles about children's language and literacy development and about the ways in which teachers can take a research perspective to young children's literate behavior in classrooms.

Acknowledgments

I wish to thank many people for contributing to the emergence of this book: Dr. Daniel P. Shepardson for his scientific expertise and his constructive feedback throughout this project; Dr. Gerald Krockover for his unflaggingly optimistic encouragement and expert guidance; Brittany Newmark for her articulate understanding of genre; Dr. Anne Haas Dyson for her eloquent teaching and her consummate respect for child writers; and Bob Sickles at Eye on Education for understanding the importance of nonfiction composition for the very young. I also wish to thank the many teachers and children who were willing to try something new while remaining themselves. I will not name them all here to protect the anonymity of the children, but I thank them profoundly. Finally—and first—I wish to thank my mother, Elsie J. Britsch, a fine and creative teacher of children who left with me the richness of moments in which she led me to teaching, to children, and to myself. They have all taught me to look beyond, and to go there.

Prologue

Sometimes people think that classroom work with nonfiction and non-narrative genres is not as creative as the fictional composing, the storytelling, that children seem to do naturally. This book argues that nonfiction composing is a highly creative process for young children—that it's a different inventive process for different children. On this view, the purpose of teaching is to appreciate as well as to illuminate what child composers bring to a task and free them to envision others. This requires composers to contribute something of themselves to the process and, in the end, to go beyond whatever we've taught them.

Research is accumulating about the development of knowledge about nonfiction genres in early childhood. Lists and labels are not the only beginnings of nonfiction literacy. In fact, if we look we'll find there's a great deal of emergent explanation, classification, and nonfiction narrative in the composing of very young children. Children reveal different perspectives through their composing responses. To offer a perspective for teachers, this book pulls together the experience of teachers and children, my own experience, and what research and theory tell us. It illustrates a different way of viewing young children's nonfiction composing, and an approach that will allow teachers to originate their own methods, appropriate to the children with whom they work.

This book is for pre-service and in-service teachers in early childhood and early elementary classrooms, preschool through grade 3. In-service teachers will find the book valuable; you know what you like about your program and what you need. Pre-service teachers, who are learning about children and curricula, will find ideas to develop a stance and to spur ideas for originating classroom activity. For both, the book suggests new ways of thinking about the theory and practice of nonfiction composition with young children.

The first chapter looks at the concept of genre as response. For young children, genres represent different ways of encountering the world and appropriating experience through symbolic media—play, drawing, talking, writing, often all of these in a given situation.

This enables child composers to express their orientations to life—an expression that is further solidified through particular shapes and ways of composing.

In play, children often create responses using elements of nonfiction and non-narrative genres. For this reason, Chapter 2 focuses on the idea of nonfiction composing as a part of play. Teaching consists of enhancing children's creation of the scenes that surround and motivate response—or genre—early on. Chapter 3 presents some of the composing choices of child composers and links these with ideas about conventional genres. The ability to recognize different shapes and purposes for nonfiction composing helps teachers to understand, guide and expand a child's composing. Chapter 4 moves from recognition to the use of nonfiction composing in classroom investigations involving young composers. It illustrates how extended lines of nonfiction composing were developed over time both by a single composer and by a group of composers. Next, Chapter 5 considers the focused reading of nonfiction—both conventional and child-created—as a dynamic and active part of nonfiction composing. Finally, Chapter 6 presents ideas for assessing children's nonfiction composing and related teacher practice without seeking comformity to a norm.

The themes that unite these chapters are (a) genre as **response**, (b) teaching as the **creation of scenes** that surround this response, (c) **questioning** as an essential element of composing, and (d) children as **composers** of nonfiction and non-narrative texts through play, talk, drawing, writing, and reading. Underlying all of these themes, though, is the idea that joy and creativity are inherently part of nonfiction and non-narrative composing with young children. Loris Malaguzzi, the education director of the District of Reggio Emilia, in Northern Italy, said:

> I believe that children expect from adults the capacity to offer joy. Without truly radiating and receiving joy, an adult cannot foster an atmosphere where children can invent and create (Goleman, Kaufman, and Ray, 1992, p. 83).

This book offers not method but mindset, a perspective for noticing the invention, valuing the complexity, and taking joy in the work of child composers. Children will show us what to teach them as long as we can learn how to see.

Chapter 1

"It's Not a *Story*"

Children Responding through Nonfiction

Introduction

When I was a preschool teacher, anxious to stimulate the children's language growth, I encouraged every bit of imagining that I saw and I fed every glimmer of expression of that imagination. During dramatic play, at the writing table, in the play yard, even at the lunch table, I would nudge, "What's happening in your story?" There was Annie with her pink clouds and crystal unicorns, Jane and her multicolored castles with "crenellations" for "Sleepin' Bootie." Then there were children like Dinah who, after a time, began to stipulate: "It's not a *story*, Susan!" So I began to watch more closely. All sorts of nonfiction literacy play were taking place in my classroom. Not all of the children in the group used fiction, or even narrative, as a primary way to get their meanings across. Not all had meanings that fiction was adequate to communicate. Annie, for example, created stories only after a period of several months during which she wrote only personal "notes" to her best friend, Lizzie. Josh's favorite early literacy products were the lists he created of toys he wanted, "estimates" of how much bike repairs would cost at his pretend fix-it shop, or

1

instructions detailing "How to Fight Dragons" for the knights in his dramatic play. Other children wrote lists of friends' names, addressed cards they had made as gifts ("To Andy from Larisa"), or played "what did I spell" games with random strings of letters. These, too, were literate activities that helped children to delineate and elaborate fields of play. But I didn't prod their invention in the same way I did the children's storytelling. I didn't recognize in these the same kind of linguistic creativity that I saw in the stories. These other forms of literacy also put forth a conception of a child's world (Bakhtin, 1981), or an immediately important piece of it, and often provoked more social activity than the storytelling. In the end, I realized that these non-stories were often more essential than fiction to a particular child's development of literacy. For this reason, I'd like to begin this chapter with a story about the growth of my own awareness of the range of genres beyond stories.

Years after Annie, Dinah, and Josh, I was giving a talk about children's nonfiction composing to a group of university faculty. By this time, I understood that some children's literacy capabilities are misinterpreted as low simply because they hate writing and reading stories. Even Mem Fox has said she "can't stand writing stories" and writes them not from her imagination but ". . . only when an idea from life or books jumps into my head" (Fox, 1993, p. 18). I, too, dislike certain kinds of stories. I have no taste for fantasy narrative. I avoid reading, too, if my entire exposure to literature had been limited to fantasy alone. Having cultivated the utmost respect for those children who would rather dive into a book about the muck at the bottom of the riverbed than one about princes and princesses, I started to search out children's "non-stories," their antifiction writing, at every opportunity. I advocated for this just as relentlessly as I had for stories. With this new preoccupation in mind, I displayed for the assembled professors the following example from Eric's kindergarten science journal.

Eric composed this piece after an autumn leaf walk. His teacher had asked the children to record their observations about change. Eric explained his journal entry: "The leaf is falling . . . falling . . . falling ('F F F'). When it gets to the bottom, it shows leaf veins ('S L V'). Then . . . compost ('C P')" (Britsch, 2001a, p. 155).

"What might we call this?" I asked my audience, anticipating

Figure 1.1 Eric's falling leaf.

that someone would peg it as a process analysis or mention its specialized vocabulary.

"It's a narrative," came the first response.

I didn't expect this answer. Eric's masterful description of decomposition—a mere *story*? But I had to admit that it was a narrative account: the story of what happens to trees in the fall. The piece did what a narrative does: it told what happened (see Gergen, 1999). But Eric's composition was a nonfiction narrative in which, using the first consonant of each syllable, he labeled the elements of his drawing to chronicle the process of decay. His accompanying oral narration made use of present-tense verbs and the example of a single leaf to represent what happens to all leaves (see Derewianka, 1990). In this, it reflected elements of a report that describes "the way things are" (Cope and Kalantzis, 1993, p. 9). But, as would a narrative, the replicated leaves in Eric's composition visually tracked a sequence, changing from green (at the top) to pencil-colored (his second leaf) to a string of alphabet letters as the leaf disintegrated into compost. Eric's talk about the leaves "falling . . . falling . . . falling" accurately and dramatically reflected this progression. All in all, however, I had seen this composition primarily as a kind of drawn-written-spoken description.

"It seems that you have a very set definition of 'genre,'" the listener observed at the end of my talk.

The charge was true, and it bothered me. In fact, I realized, Eric's leaf composition couldn't be pigeonholed. It represented his knowledge and his experience in more than one way as he stood these up against the new context of the leaf walk. Still, I thought I'd understood what a genre was: "regularly recurring situations . . . accompanied by language, of whatever kind . . ." which "give rise to regularities in the texts which are produced in that situation" (Kress, 1993, p. 27). A prayer was a genre. So was a novel. A set of instructions. Different genres followed specific and differentiated forms; in other words, each was codified, clear, distinct.

But what about the birthday card that one four-year-old had given me on *her* birthday? "BIRTHDA CACONT," she had written, and then read to me while giggling: "Birthday cake on teacher's head!"

This was a card, a gift, a joke, a power play—a child-created way of participating in a situation. I had to conclude then that genres are not straitjackets. There's no one-to-one match between a purpose and a form. What, then, *is* genre?

What Is Genre?

For me, the most useful way to conceptualize "genre" is to view it as a response. Especially for young children, perhaps genres are best viewed as different ways of encountering the world and staking a claim to it through symbolic media. The claims staked by different children reflect their involvement in particular situations—both social and pedagogical—although these two should usually intersect.

I show my students, pre-service teachers, piece after piece produced by very young children who *are* involved in situations—emotional situations, play situations, classroom situations—in

Figure 1.2 "Birthday cake on teacher's head!"

which they use different combinations of play, drawing, writing, and talk to do many things: to tell jokes, to fit a science activity into their own frame of reference, to give "estimates" that might crack open the window of friendship. Gunther Kress (1993) says that children's textual representations may contain elements of several genres, combined in different ways by different children. The social world gives rise to situated texts that may begin to form frames—genres. Because composers—both adults and children—carry out many purposes at once in their compositions, we can't even say that they are mixing genres. This would mean that we've identified a stable set of genres that can be mixed (Kress, 1999).

"That's OK for younger kids," some object. "But what about the older ones? Don't you have to make them write about certain things so they learn it?"

I don't think so. No one learns anything by being made to do it for someone else's reason. We teach by creating scenes, sets of contexts in which children can practice questioning, arguing, remembering, projecting through writing, talking, drawing, and acting. These scenes contribute to the personal histories of individuals in relationship with others, scenes in which the child constructs and uses ideas about self and others. Language, shaped into a range of genres, emerges in response to these scenes. This can happen in classrooms. Do I have a lesson plan that will assure it? A sequence that will "work" every time? No. But teaching is not a set of procedures; it's a set of relationships.

Developing Knowledge about Genre

How do children learn about genre? Do they learn to fill a shape or do they first create the fill? Contrasting fiction and non-fiction, Helen Benedict makes the following statement about adult readers:

> Nonfiction is always dependent on what can be found out and verified, and it is always limited by the private, the secret, the unrealized, and the unarticulated. Nonfiction always keeps the reader on the outside. Perhaps this is why some readers prefer nonfiction—perhaps they are, in a sense, hiding. The distance between reader and subject in nonfiction is so much greater than in fiction that perhaps it feels safer. After all, it is easier to read about the suffering of the Other than to be pulled into feeling it oneself (1999, p. 49).

By implication, it's the exterior life that concerns the nonfiction writer, not the interior life. Although this admittedly large generalization may be true for adult writers, I found myself examining Benedict's statement in terms of child writers of nonfiction and coming to quite a different conclusion. For young children, nonfiction doesn't mean being on the outside. It isn't hiding. It *is* very much interior. It is a taking-in. This has something to tell us about how we help children to develop their genre knowledge.

Children's drawing, talk, and writing project the meanings they differentiate, and connect these with aspects of the whole that the child is becoming. Of course, for very young children, this begins in play (see, for instance, Morrow, 1997; Owocki, 1999; Schickendanz, 1999). In the context of imaginative play, children convey a great deal of information by means of nonfiction and non-narrative forms. What I suggest is a different way of looking at or interpreting this play. Through real world, factual topics that children enact and in which they are interested—whether zoo animal, bank teller, or pharmacist—children make a claim on certain

Fiction and Nonfiction, Narrative and Non-narrative

Narrative comprises a large number of genres, but all *narratives* tell stories. The stories may be real, as in a biography, or unreal, as in fairy tales. *Fictional narrative* often draws upon the real world and depicts contexts that are familiar to the writer. In this respect, fiction and nonfiction share the same playing field. In fact, fiction is usually set in the real world. Fictional events, however, are events that didn't happen. Fiction is a much smaller category than nonfiction; it includes no exposition, no argument, no analysis. Nonfiction includes all of that. Fiction is artifice created through characterization, setting, dialogue that didn't actually occur. Specialized genres, such as fantasy or science fiction, even contain entities that can exist only in one's imagination. But fictional narrative is still truth—a true way of perceiving the world for the composer, as is nonfiction.

Nonfiction, however, can also be narrative. An example of this would be a chronicle of a scientist's investigation:

> One scientist saw a long line of caterpillars . . . Then he had an idea. He put some of them on the edge of a glass bowl. Around and around they went, following each other's trail in a circle for days and days. They never stopped or climbed down. They just kept on playing follow-the-leader until the scientist took them off (Rood, 1960, p. 11).

Whether it's wholly or partially narrative, nonfiction exists only in a real context. The question is, "Did it happen?" If it happened, it's nonfiction.

Non-narrative genres, on the other hand, don't tell a story. They may argue, they may describe, they may analyze, they may list, but they don't tell a story. Non-narrative writing is usually nonfictional, although a fictional narrative may use non-narrative devices (e.g., a list of ingredients for the witch's brew, a map for finding the treasure). Not all nonfiction, however, is non-narrative and not all narrative is fiction.

kinds of information, certain chunks of the world, and represent this using emergent nonfiction and non-narrative tools. Episodes of play and of the pedagogical activity in classrooms involve the construction and use of genres that relate to the children's own involvement as participants in specific social worlds. This is constantly transformative as children engage in experience in different ways.

So, for young children, genres represent different ways of appropriating experience, observation, and action through symbolic media: drawing, talking, writing—often all three in any given situation. Children reshape these, using their developing capacities, based on the requirements of the situation. This is not a normative process. As Vygotsky has pointed out, the developmental history of written language,

> . . . does not follow a single direct line in which something like a clear continuity of forms is maintained . . . Its line of development seems to disappear altogether; then suddenly, as if from nowhere, a new line begins, and at first it seems that there is absolutely no continuity between the old and the new (Vygotsky, 1978, p. 106).

Nonetheless, some of the research has viewed lists and labels as forms that precede more sophisticated expository forms of writing. Tom Newkirk (e.g., 1987, 1989) has pointed out that expository competence develops as students build upon early labeling, such as making signs and lists. These are intermediate forms that children try out as they move toward the more integrated forms of exposition (such as explanation, classification) that are needed during the later school years. Ten years later, Zecker (1999) found that, although the K–1 children she researched used emergent writing forms, they also demonstrated a great deal of knowledge about the specific characteristics of a given genre as evidenced by their readings of self-created texts. In Zecker's study, the list was the genre children knew best. Their knowledge about the content and style of letters and stories was not as well developed.

In contrast, Kamberelis (1999) found that children in one K–2 classroom knew more about the rules and conventions of narrative than they did about poems or reports. He found lots of "hybrid genres" (p. 422) in response to report-writing and poem-writing tasks but, at the same time, some of the younger children produced the best-formed fictional narratives, science reports, and poems. Kamberelis observed that there was a great deal of uniqueness in the ways that the children organized their knowledge about genre, concluding that genre learning is quite complex and probably takes place over several years.

Unlike Kamberelis, Donovan found that when K–5 students were asked to write about a familiar topic, most (over 80 percent) wrote an informational text. Still, Donovan also found that children at all grade levels frequently composed attribute lists—random listings of two or more facts about a single topic (Donovan, 2001). They used these as informational texts; however, Donovan emphasized not viewing labeling as the beginning of writing. Over half of the kindergartners and first graders in her study produced texts more complex than labels or lists for both story and informational prompts.

For a number of years, though, writing and reading in elementary school classrooms focused heavily on children's stories. Researchers and teacher-researchers also valued children's oral, written, and dramatized narratives as the primary forum for the expression of developing literacy capacities (e.g., Britsch, 1992; Cooper, 1993; Dyson, 1989; Paley, 1981; Rowe, 1994). In fact, while American schoolchildren may have quite a bit of intuitive knowledge about "story," they are not as fluent in the nonfiction genres—persuasion, explanation, information, description, and analysis (Moss, Leone, and Dipillo, 1997). The *NAEP Writing Report Card for the Nation and the States* recently showed that only 9 percent of fourth graders could write skillful informative pieces, and only 10 percent could produce skillful persuasive writing (Greenwald, Persky, Campbell, and Mazzeo, 1999, p. 132). Even fewer, 2 percent, could compose *excellent* informative and persuasive pieces of writing. The National Association for the Education of Young Children (NAEYC) now cites familiarity with "stories and other kinds of text" as an appropriate early literacy focus (Neuman, Copple, and Bredekamp, 2000, p. 70). Still, although familiarity with "narrative and informational stories" (Neuman, Copple, and Bredekamp, 2000, p. 21) is given as an appropriate literacy focus for first graders, literacy experiences for preschool and kindergarten children are often confined to story reading—not writing.

I don't believe that we need to see stories as the primary form of literate activity for all children. Neither do we need to reduce children's writing to lists. There's an abundance of emergent explanation, chronicling and decomposition of processes, classification—and more—in the nonfiction and non-narrative composing of young children. When children begin composing, the language they use is varied and vibrant. Instead of proceeding to encyclopedic renderings of someone else's thought, writing should actually become more contextualized, more embedded in children's lives as they find new ways to capture their experiences (Dyson,

1988). Dyson points out that children's imaginative writing is more than "text worlds with beginnings, middles, and ends"; it also engages children in the discovery of "ways of understanding their own experiences and of connecting with others" (1988, p. 32). This "writing of one's story is not simply making words visible on paper, but enacting worlds" (Dyson, 1990, p. 11). Nonfiction as a response also engages the composer's interior life. Some children grab hold of the world they see and reflect it back in ways other than what we call "stories."

The Horizontal Curriculum

Today, I abandoned my classroom for a spot outdoors where my students, pre-service kindergarten teachers, sat under three different kinds of trees: a crabapple, an evergreen, and an oak.

"What," I asked them, "can children learn from these three trees?"

To begin, one student pointed out that two of the trees had leaves of different shapes and that the other tree had needles. We categorized these and described them as "deciduous" and "evergreen." Another student noticed the items that fell from the trees: acorns, crabapples, pinecones. This led us to the creatures that consume acorns, squirrels, and then to the question of whether crabapples are, in fact, apples that are consumable by humans. And where do the squirrels live? Are their nests like those of birds? Here we had already represented at least three curricular areas: science, math, and language arts.

In this same way, the horizontal thinking children do combines a range of subject areas all at the same time because, as David Elkind points out, "there are no sharp boundaries separating their various types of knowledge" (1987, p. 108). We can reflect this kind of thinking in our curricula by helping children to make the most of these links between kinds of knowledge instead of separating them into subject matter categories. Elkind argues these are not terribly meaningful for children. For example, literacy—talk, drawing, and writing—combines quite readily with science, even for very young children. Given the chance, kindergartners can and do construct and convey their understandings about science phenomena through child-created science journals that they use in situated classroom science activities (Shepardson and Britsch, 1997).

Eric's science journal composition about the falling leaves was produced the day that he and the other seventeen children in his kindergarten took a nature walk with their teacher (Britsch, 2001a). Throughout the walk, the teacher had drawn the children's attention to items outdoors that had changed over time. She picked up a number of decaying leaves and pointed out their veins, explaining that these remained as the leaf changed from its live, green state to a decayed one. The children collected some examples of things that had changed and brought them back to the classroom. Ellen brought back a skeletonized leaf. The class looked at a wild onion and talked about how an onion could be found growing in the park. Deanna brought back a piece of asphalt from the street adjacent to the park where they had walked. Jake added a comment about dinosaur bones.

Next, the teacher announced that the children were going to use their science journals to show some of the changes they had observed. About the items the children had collected, she said, "Draw some things about how they were. What has happened? How did it get the way it looks?" She wrote, "What changed?" on the blackboard. But not everyone drew, wrote, or talked about changes they had observed.

For Deanna, the meaning of "change" resided in the chunk of asphalt she had picked up. The meaning on her journal page was carried not by written language but by a detailed drawing of the chunk itself, including black and white spots pitting the surface

---

Emergent Science Literacy

Kindergarten science activities may last from two to three days. On day 1, the children participate in a whole-group discussion about what they already knew about the science phenomenon in question. Then they move to the classroom tables where, seated in groups of four, they draw or write about this prior knowledge in individual science journals. On day 2, the children engage in practice at their tables or on outings outside the classroom; here, they explore the topic using manipulative materials or in outdoor activities through which they gather artifacts that exemplify the topic or phenomenon. Then they return to their tables in the classroom and again draw or write in their journals about what they've learned about the phenomenon. Finally, those children who wish to do so can share their findings and their journal pages as "Super Scientists" in a whole-group sharing time. The Super Scientist gets to wear a grown-up-sized white shirt, appropriately accessorized for a scientist.

of the asphalt. Another element that contributed to the change Deanna saw was a construction worker with a mustache. He had put down the yellow traffic cones Deanna had drawn, "to keep people from getting hurt." For this child author, what had changed was the street she usually crossed (Britsch, 2001a, p. 157).

Deanna developed her interpretation of change by using oral language, drawing, and a little invented spelling to tell a story, to create a scene containing some logical but imagined elements, but it was based on reality. Isn't this what novelists do? Martin, however, contends that imaginative writing distracts students from building scientific understandings because it does not explore the way in which science interprets the world. Narrative does not classify, decompose, measure, or explain (Martin, 1993, p. 199).

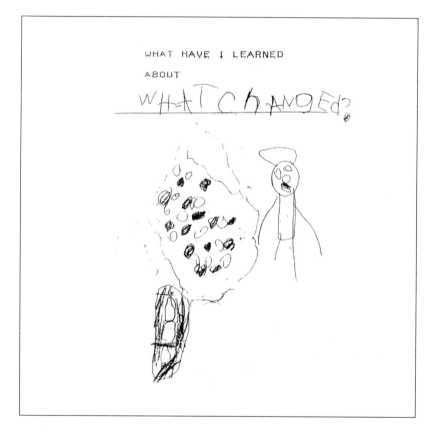

Figure 1.3 Deanna's montage.

Deanna's composition is really a pretty sophisticated linking of one context with an idea, an abstract concept. She's designed an explanation, a descriptive account, a bit of fiction—a multi-genre piece (Romano, 2000)—to convey an idea by drawing on the resources she had. What is paramount: should we change her narrative to something more standard, more one-dimensional? But Deanna will turn away now if we try to change her piece into a science report. Her montage makes sense of her experience.

The pieces we judge as "better" may just happen to be closer to something we recognize than Deanna's composition. The question is whether we're teaching children to choose from a set of tools to convey their understanding, or simply teaching them to imitate forms at prescribed times.

Nick, on the other hand, had a long-range historical view of change. A previous unit on dinosaurs and fossils suggested to him a set of creatures that no longer exist. He included two representatives of this world in his piece: a tyrannosaurus rex (labeled "T") and an ankylosaurus. Both were labeled "D" and indicated with arrows.

Nick contrasted this scene with one containing a person waiting to cross the street at a traffic light (Britsch, 2001a, p. 156). He provided temporal labels for each world, each scene: "50000 YERS AGO" for the dinosaurs and "TODAY" for the contemporary scene. Nick's composition depicts the beginning and the current phase, the end, of a process, unlike Eric's leaf composition, which accounts for the entire process either through drawing or writing. Nick understands that all parts of a change need not be observable. Both he and Deanna had included known but nonobservable elements in their depictions of "change." Neither Nick's account nor Eric's, on the other hand, are explanations in the way that Deanna's page attempts to explain the presence of certain elements of her scene. In one sense, they are stories, narrative accounts. But they are all very much more.

Back in the classroom after the leaf walk, the teacher "lectured" briefly about air, light, and water as she pointed to a large picture of a tree. Sam paced back and forth just outside the perimeter of the circle and appeared uninterested. Then he stopped still and began to speak.

"Hey!" he said, "maybe this spring we could— um um—while it's turning green—then we could bring it to school and THEN we could show the class how it's turning *green*!

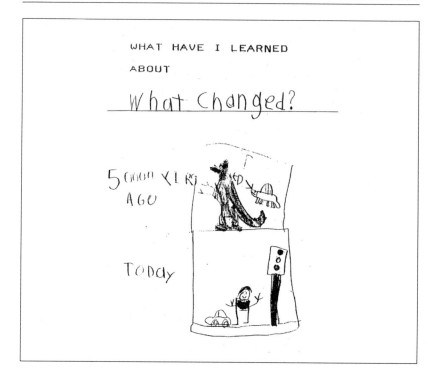

Figure 1.4 Nick's dinosaurs.

"Sam," the teacher asked, "what if we take the leaf off the tree and we bring it in. Would it still work?"

"Yes . . . well . . . I guess it would NOT work . . . I just *remembered*, class!"

Standing, he turned to face the class. "Cause the tree would be giving the leaf oxygen . . . cause see the tree would be giving the leaf food and then the leaf would just die!"

He started to pace and he began to motion with his hands while talking. Facing the seated class, he announced, "If we pick the leaf off the tree this spring then it will just <u>die</u>. So we have to go out to the tree and we have to <u>look</u> at the leaf so—if we're gonna do this <u>really big</u>, we're gonna have to bring a whole tree to the classroom . . . and do you think that would be easy? NO!"

He threw up his hands and then began a chopping motion.

His teacher continued, "If you chop the tree down, would it work?"

"No!" he concluded, as if this reply were now self-evident.

Approaching the chart of the tree, he began to trace the trunk and continued, "The food comes down here . . . and it goes underground and then it comes up into the tree."

Sam traced from the roots up to the leaves of the tree (Britsch, 2001b, pp. 112–113).

Sam's talk was highly technical. Through his monologue, he built a nonfiction narrative including a cause-and-effect explanation of plant growth, albeit an inaccurate one. He delivered this as something he was teaching the other children. He actually did more than had Eric in his leaf composition: Sam tried to build an explanation. His graphic activity, however, was very imaginative: Air Man, Water Man, and Light Man "wiggled" into the tree, he

Figure 1.5 Sam's journal entry: tree growth.

said, to feed its leaves. His oral language had been much more complex and had involved abstracting from the teacher's explanation to very logical explanation focused on an abstract "tree." On his journal page, he simply labeled the elements of this explanation by anthropomorphizing them (Britsch, 2001b, p. 114). Why? We can speculate that it's because of the difficulty for a kindergartner of representing this kind of abstract content on paper. Air Man, Water Man, and Light Man make the central elements of the process concrete. For Sam, this level of explanation was an oral genre.

Children combine many oral and written language functions in their compositions. Some are more conventional and others are much more child-originated. Children respond to experience in ways that are intrinsically horizontal. It is impossible to separate the elements of explanation from those of memoir, elements of science from those of language. Each is necessary to the life of the other. So for young children genre is not first a form; it is, in fact, a purpose or a collection of purposes. Of course, genres can also be oral (the story of the time the cooling fan in my computer stopped and fried the hard drive,) or written (an account of Einstein's invention of relativity); (Overbye, 2000). Rarely, though, do we find one purpose alone in the literate work of either children or adults. For this reason, all of the lines in Table 1.1 are dotted ones. It's often difficult to set up a one-to-one correspondence between genre and purpose.

Still, in higher education, divisions such as description, exposition, argumentation, narration, persuasion, and poetry require this kind of specification (Winterowd and Blum, 1994). On the other hand, narrative accounts of science investigations can be, and frequently are, composed. Giving someone directions around a city usually requires some description of landmarks, neighborhoods, and streets. A single genre, such as a letter, can describe, argue, persuade, or simply send information.

Our classroom literacy curricula can mirror this mix and take advantage of its spread as we offer elements that will expand the set of choices within the scope of each child's awareness. In the long run, this lets the child control the language, not the other way around. It also means sharing the power with child writers themselves. This informs us as teachers and energizes our response to the children.

Response opportunities like the journal pages shown here reflect the kind of horizontal thinking that children do. It is by

Table 1.1 Some Oral and Written Nonfiction Genres

GENRE/PURPOSE	ORAL	WRITTEN
Narrative nonfiction	Anecdote (e.g., computer meltdown story)	Biography; memoir
Argument (rhetorical)	A discussion in which one contends that one artist is less noteworthy than another	Newspaper letter to the editor
Description	Weather report	Classified ad
Recount	"Headline news"; court testimony	Historical account
Procedure (Green, 1992) / How-to (Martin, 1993)	How to get from one building to another on a university campus; how to customize software or use a new e-mail system	Recipe; computer manuals; instructions with an unassembled product (e.g., how to put together a porch swing)
Letters/notes	Voice-mail messages	E-mail (often telegraphic or quasi-oral in style); office memos
Explanation	Explaining why magnets attract. (This is different from simply listing the things that do and do not attract)	A letter ending a relationship; an explanation of the second law of thermodynamics
Report (e.g., Derewianka, 1990; Green, 1992)	A presentation given in a class (perhaps extemporaneously)	Science journal article; informational pamphlet

means of this kind of thought that children derive interpretations of science experience, for example, going beyond simply recounting a series of observations. Children's own nonfiction writing is not just about what can be "found out and verified;" nonfiction is not just the empirical (Benedict, 1999, p. 49). Nonfiction is not so distant from young children. The development of nonfiction genres draws directly on an interior life. Children see what is there and they must relate it to what is not there. These kindergartners, for example, pulled the visible, external source of their science experiences into the internal contexts of their own experience, their thinking processes, their interests, and their own literacy capacities (Ochs, Taylor, Rudolph, and Smith, 1992). Each child reinterpreted the immediate experience on the journal page in a different way and pulled the activity closer.

A Plea for the Unconventional

Research is accumulating about the development of genre knowledge in children. What to do with this information in early childhood and elementary classrooms? Christine Pappas and Barbara Pettegrew have argued that we should veer away from a focus on "teacher-directed transmission of text types" (Pappas and Pettegrew, 1998, p. 42). They insist that work with nonfiction genres not be limited to teaching children mechanical patterns, or creating genre templates to be filled in on cue. "Real writers," Mark Wiley points out, "must decide what they will compose based on their intentions, who will read their texts, and what effects they want their texts to have on these real and projected readers" (2000, p. 64). This means, he says, that students need the capability to express themselves to readers in order to achieve purposes of their own—and not just those of their teachers.

At the very beginning of this process, young children do not simply reproduce convention, so why limit them to this? As teachers, we can create an atmosphere where this kind of creative process can happen throughout the curriculum, where children feel respected enough to express their own ideas, and not as a result of tasks that funnel them toward one inevitable answer. Long ago, Moffett (1968) complained that genre divisions simply satisfy a passion for taxonomy—for hierarchies and lists. Genres constitute a hazard, he said, because they make teachers and students feel they have to define what a short story is by tracing the similarities between a set of examples. This, he said, only results in a reduction that doesn't help anyone to read, write, or appreciate. In other words, simply having information about what the conventions are, sticking to my "set definition" of genre, and holding children to one purpose isn't enough. Donovan (2001) suggests a developmental approach; although she contends that labels are not the beginnings of literacy, she says that if they are viewed as such by teachers, then teachers may aim for mere labeling and "disregard" unconventionally written texts (p. 440). Teachers might, instead, simply focus on helping children to label pictures.

I, too, advocate paying *more* attention to the unconventionally written texts. There's more of the child in them. We can discover more of what the child is working on there—what the child has noticed and how these elements are linked to a context. What we learn from research might be reduced to a normative set of beginning, intermediate, and conventional forms. Instead, we could use this information more productively to heighten our own awareness of the kinds of choices that are available to children in a given situation so we can help them to construct an expanded set to draw on. This means that, in addition to knowledge about the conventional forms, teachers also need to learn about genres from children. Over time, we would hope for more complexly organized structures, but what is complexity at any particular developmental moment for any particular child? The thinking processes and the action underlying genre use have to be woven into activity that is useful to the child instead of being presented in terms of isolated forms that the child merely imitates. As Piaget put it, "Learning that is not the result of the child's own activity will be deformed" (Piaget, cited in Duckworth, 1964).

In their play, children take in the outer world and they use the literacy artifacts that are necessary to perpetuate this play. Nonfiction genres, too, are ways of perpetuating activity—ways that are organic to that activity for its participants. Different children will make different connections. The question is, how does literacy relate to the sense-making process for that child? How does the child *make* it make sense? We're comfortable with this when it comes to storytelling; somehow the shutter slams shut when we leave the world of fiction.

Chapter 2

"'I Hope You Feel Better' and Raindrops and Rain Clouds"—

Nonfiction Composition in the Play of Young Children

The Beginnings of Nonfiction: Composing as Gesture

Play is at the heart of it. In play, children communicate their personal intentions to each other, and they incorporate nonfiction literacy into this communication. Vygotsky spoke of gestures—physical movement itself—as "writing in air" and of writing as gestures that have become fixed. "The gesture," he wrote, "is the initial visual sign that contains the child's future writing as an acorn contains a future oak" (1978, p. 107). For example, Jason (age two years, nine months: 2:9) made the following gesture on his paper with a marker:

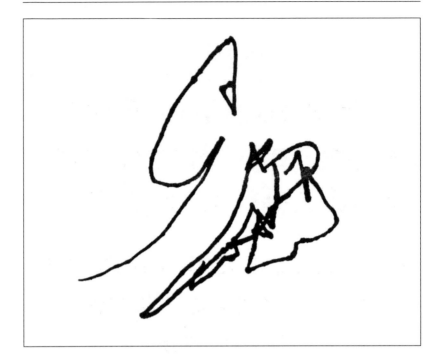

Figure 2.1 Jason's "flying airplane."

When asked about his page, Jason explained: "This is a flying airplane."

This was a meaning, a very personal meaning that he conveyed through the physical movement of his marker on the page. We can't say that he necessarily set out to represent this specific object, an airplane, but he interpreted his piece after having *felt* the upward swoop that represents the central quality of an airplane for him. So this wasn't primarily a drawing of a *thing*; it was a gesture. Altogether, the effect was to convey the impression of flying, of wings, of arcing upward. This was play, and the beginnings of the graphic encoding of meaning.

Jason's airplane could have been a fictional one; it was certainly an abstract plane, in the sense that there was no airplane (toy or real) in the room. But we can't immediately label this piece a "story." It was a composition made of gesture, drawing, and talk that he related to what he knew of the world. Both fiction and nonfiction have their roots here. We'll have to wait and see where Jason takes it from here.

Along with these physically gestural beginnings of written language, children also make what may be called *social gestures* in the context of their composing play (Britsch, 1988). In other words, children create written products to symbolize and carry out real-world social relationships in the context of play. The next sections will describe several classroom scenes that illustrate the oral and graphic (written or drawn) media as well as the corresponding social gestures that the child composers are making.

Parties

One warm day five girls (ranging in age from 3:7 to 4:3) decided to have a party outdoors during playtime. On the landing of a short stairway that led inside, they spread out dolls and dishes—the guests and utensils for their party. They got out a bucket of scarves and draped these over the banisters on either side of the stairway. The most significant scarf was the long one that they draped across the lowest step: their blockade.

Next, they went over to the outdoor writing table, where they made several "notes" on two-by-two-inch Post-its. They took these back to their party space and stuck them to the banisters. The notes are shown in Figure 2.2. The girls read each of the notes, respectively, as follows:

"Party."

"We love parties."

"Party things."

Two of the notes said: "NO BOYS ALLOWED!"

The girls reinforced the posting of their notes with many loud statements to the effect that no boys were, in fact, allowed at the party. Predictably, after about five minutes, two boys approached. The girls immediately shouted, "NO BOYS ALLOWED!"

In response, Darrin (3:11) inched even closer, stopping just at the borderline—just before he provoked any more shouts. He had been sitting at the writing table making a card for his mother on a large piece of white construction paper folded in half. This he carried to a more central spot, opened it, held it up to his face, and read: "Our newspaper says, 'No parties allowed today!'"

This announcement provoked no perceptible change. So Darrin raised the page again and read, more emphatically: "MY newspaper says, 'NO PARTIES TODAY!'"

The girls failed to acknowledge this dictum as well, so Darrin

Figure 2.2 Party warnings.

returned to the writing table and transformed his newspaper back into a card for his mother, presumably a more receptive audience.

These children used written products falling into quite appropriate genres in order to take action in their social lives. They used both the notes and the newspaper to reflect and emphasize the social reality they wished to enforce. These weren't stories. Essentially, they were emergent rhetorical pieces that argued the writer's view of the world and aimed to pull others into it.

No one suggested any of this activity to the children, although they had been using Post-its for several weeks as a way to send notes to others in the class. Senders would find the recipient's name on a big two- by three-foot note board and post the note beside that name. Recipients would simply find their own names. The children could either dictate their notes or write by themselves. The term *"write"* was defined by the children themselves; some used what Marie Clay calls "linear mock writing" (1975, p. 48), each piece identified by a personal writing style different from anyone else's. Some children drew pictures that were clearly distinct from their writing; others simply wrote their names or used the word-initial consonants that were significant to them. One two-year-old girl dictated a note to a two-year-old boy in the group: "Dear Gabriel, I love a horsey."

Gabriel dictated his response: "Dear Horsey, I want a horsey for my birthday."

With "Dear Horsey," Gabriel might have been joking or he might simply have remembered the last word in the note. He knew who had sent the note, and his response did coincide with the meaning that writer had found most important: "horsey." Note getters might ask note writers to read their notes, but it was often enough just to find a tangible gift from someone else who had thought enough to give it.

The children soon transformed the tool of the note into much more dynamic and immediate vehicles for their social relationships, as in the party scene. These notes communicated a personal intention, shared by the group of girls. I did not try to mold the notes into conventional forms or enforce the need for a response on paper; genre as response is, first, a need. Like Jason's airplane, the notes were compositions of talk, social action, and very early written meanings. They were not stories, but nonfiction compositions. I offer this as a way to view children's talk, play, drawing, reading and pretend reading, and emergent writing about factual topics. We may see composing in labels, lists, diagrams, charts, drawings of familiar scenes, and dictated exposition that graphically display children's perceptions of their experiences. For example, the children in the group also composed tickets using linear mock writing to get into the hospital (i.e., the outdoor playhouse). In order to get in with a patient (a doll), you had to present a ticket. As needed, more tickets were made at the outdoor writing table from index cards, adding machine tape, notepad pages—any small piece of paper.

When the hospital became a store, the tickets became receipts. When handing a receipt to a customer, for example, Laura would explain the procedure that went with it: "This is your receipt. You have to come again someday, but not when it's closed." Unlike the party notes, the linear mock writing on the tickets had no specific meaning—at least not a meaning that was revealed to me as the teacher. The tickets did require writing, however, to legitimate the piece of paper as a ticket, so this writing fixed the social gesture of including ticket holders and receipt getters in the group of patients or customers. The tickets generally reinforced the theme of activity in public places and the need for the print products used in those real-world contexts. The children incorporated this non-narrative composing into play scenes that were works of the imagination. They may also have helped to carry on the story of a particular relationship in the context of that imaginative play. Like fiction, the events involved real-world settings, but they didn't actually happen. This makes a larger point about genre itself: it's not absolute. There are no clear divisions between genre domains, as we saw in Chapter 1 with Eric's falling leaf composition.

As the school year continued, the children in the "ticket" group began to notice and produce more conventional symbols: letters of the alphabet. Although these evolving forms now became part of their compositions, the purposes for these compositions (the nature of their responses) remained quite stable. One day, for example, Laura (aged 4;3) presented me with a note-gift: a large "S" that she had written on a small sheet of paper. A dictated message accompanied the gift: "This is for you. It's a 'S.' You can take it home. You could hang it up in your room."

In many ways Laura's gift— the first letter of my name—was much the same as a picture of me; it was a first order symbol (Vygotsky, 1978). For Laura, "S" simply represented *me*, but she was beginning to realize that her own written meanings could

The Writing Table

One center or station can be designated as the "writing table," available daily for at least 30 to 45 minutes. Writing, of course, includes the drawing, talking, writing, and dictating, as well as the reading, of children's compositions. If the writing table is adjacent to the dramatic play area, the children can make use of writing and drawing implements in their dramatic play. Writing table materials may correlate with the current theme in the dramatic play area, but most often the children's own spontaneous ideas for the available materials will prove more fruitful than anything we can invent!

Store the writing and drawing materials in a set of permanent or portable shelves near the writing table. Or simply provide supplies sorted into baskets on the table. In any case, be sure to vary the kinds of supplies provided on at least a weekly basis, or as new inspirations become urgent. (One day, for example, I bought a sunflower on the way to school and simply placed it in the middle of the writing table for the children to examine, touch, and respond to as they wished.) Some other ideas:

- odds and ends: colored cellophane, bits of wrapping paper, blank sticky labels of different sizes, small pieces of fabric, envelopes, rubber stamps and stamp pads, old business cards, discarded business forms
- blank books of different sizes made from several sheets of plain white paper folded in half and bound by your sewing machine (basting stitch). Lined pages can be used later as dictated by the children's developmental needs.
- different textures and sizes of paper
- a tape dispenser and different colors of tape
- a hole punch
- scissors
- pads and tablets of varying sizes (long narrow tablets for lists, small tablets for tiny writing, large and small college blue books for book-length products)
- rolls of adding-machine tape
- pencils, both standard and large size. (Pencils alone may tend to suggest writing instead of drawing.)
- markers and/or crayons. (The availability of color—or not—will provoke different uses for the writing materials and different kinds of detail in the children's products.)

become gifts to another. Like the tickets, this non-narrative composition had a function within a real-world relationship. Laura might not have been able to tell me how the shape—"S"—sounded on its own or even that it was the first sound in my name, but she was on the cusp of understanding something that is crucial to literacy: "one can draw not only things but also speech" (Vygotsky, 1978, p. 115). In this respect, Laura's nonfiction composition took her much further than would any number of story starters I might have provided.

Josh

Josh was three years and nine months old at the beginning of the school year. During the first months of the year, Josh spent a large portion of his outside playtime talking to the adults in the yard—to my co-teacher and me. He was very affectionate, and would often gaze up at us and say, "I wove you." If someone else said it first, he shied off while smiling joyously at the ground.

Josh had a very quick mind and a memory like an elephant. He readily made connections between facts or stories from books that were read to him and the events he observed. It was almost possible to see the wheels turning—or *whirling*—filing new facts away in his mind for future use. Mostly, he loved to talk and he loved to play out roles that he adopted: Batman, Robin Hood, "Darth Vader *the Good*." It was through these roles that he con-

---

Outdoor Drawing and Writing

To accompany an indoor writing table, available daily, use an outdoor area as a casual writing/drawing center when weather permits. Children can sit together in the sun, chatting and writing with various degrees of intensity. Sometimes they'll work on products that become gifts to other children, elements of dramatic play situations, or any number of purposes.

Create portable individual desks by turning a cardboard box upside down. (Boxes for printer paper are a good size.) Cut out handles big enough for a child's hand on either end of the box. Cut out a circular space in one corner of the top of the box. Sink a clean yogurt container into this cutout to hold pencils, crayons, markers, and scissors. This way, the children have the tools they need as they compose. The children can group the desks or work individually in whatever location they desire.

Children's activity often blossoms during outdoor writing times with the availability of more space for activity and play structures that may lend themselves to dramatic play. This can translate into more space for personal creativity.

nected with other children—usually within imaginative contexts that he set up. One of his first was his "fix-it shop." When some remodeling work was done at a neighbor's home, Josh had watched a series of carpenters visit and make estimates on the job. He began to carry around a pad and pencil. At school, he'd get out the plastic carpenter tools and lay them out near the tricycle area for his shop. Other children would ride their bikes over and stop. He'd kneel down, examine the vehicle, and scrunch up his face. Tapping his pencil on his chin, he'd write down his estimate on a pad of paper in linear mock writing. Then he'd tear off the estimate and give it to the customer, who would ride away. Josh rarely asked his customers to actually bring back their bikes so he could fix them: as he said, he just gave out estimates.

There wasn't much chat as long as the customers did as they were supposed to: ride their bikes in and leave when Josh was finished. What the fix-it shop supplied was the presence of several things that he loved: machines, pencils and pads of paper, and the enactment of the real, grown-up process that went with them. The estimates, however, represented only one of the genres in his composing repertoire. His letters were another genre. For example, one oral-written letter expressed his chagrin at a teacher's absence. Specifically, he missed the miniature road machines she often brought to school. Josh wrote the letter, shown in figure 2.3, as he talked. Unlike his estimates, he read the letter aloud very slowly and deliberately, including intonational emphases that set off salient syntactic units—sentences:

> Dear *Millie*, would you like ta come over to my house some*day*. You could bring your machines with *you*. We can go to the *park*. Dear Millie from *Josh*.

Visually, he separated the letter into discrete sections. The salutation was small and horizontal, at the upper left. The body, the longest and most central conveyer of meaning, took up the center of the paper with larger flourishes. The closing came at the far right, unconnected to the body. Josh used his estimates and his letters quite consciously as part of particular processes he was carrying out. His genres operated on the real-world level of relationships even as they replicated non-narrative genres from real-world contexts that could actually occur (i.e., the fix-it shop) as well as fantasy contexts that exist only in the imagination (i.e., the knight training mentioned in Chapter 1).

Figure 2.3 Josh's letter to Millie.

Other children also engaged with nonfiction or non-narrative genres through dramatic play scenes. Josh's friend Dinah (3;11) began a series of play scenes (including Josh) in which she enacted a "zoo vet." One day the stuffed elephant got sick. In the middle of examining him with the plastic doctor kit, Dinah ran to the writing table, wrote "MES" on a scrap of paper, hurried back and taped it to the elephant. She pronounced "medicine" as "mE:sn," with the "n" barely audible. She had managed to induce a sound-symbol correspondence that enabled her to accomplish her medicine-giving task on both a physical and a literate level. She said, as the zoo vet, that she had to give the elephant his "medicine." To dramatize this, she borrowed a real-world non-narrative genre that served her purpose. Although also a nonfiction genre in real-life contexts, the prescription functioned fictively in Dinah's play scene.

This was play—the principal medium for learning in an early childhood classroom. Teachers can certainly take these opportunities to bring children's attention to the encoding of written language, sound-symbol connections. More importantly, however, these nonfiction compositions help the teacher to see into the child, not in terms of psychological motives, but to follow the development of the genres children use to understand their experiences and contact others. It is important to note that it's the *children* who structure these literate interactions, not the teacher. For example, as I watched Josh train the other "knights" with his instruction book, I also saw the nature of his graphic products change. I realized that he needed the freedom to expand the range of his literate purposes; he needed acceptance as a creator of both real and imaginary worlds—whatever their nature.

In a sense, every child is a Josh because every child needs a listener who knows his world. Every child needs situations that allow pencil and paper to become more familiar as tools of expression. This must be combined with face-to-face attention to oral expression. Every child needs a teacher to suggest, and to let that child suggest, verbal, social, and physical contexts that promote the exchange of what is inner with that which is outer, just as adult composers do. These discoveries take place in moments of contact between individuals. Here, immediately expressed but long-developing needs are crystallized, and the communicative tools that meet these needs can be offered.

Dinah and Amy

As children's literacy capacities develop, their nonfiction composing helps to situate friends with respect to each other, as does written language in its more mature forms. Just as Jason's airplane was linked with a physical gesture, children's composing products also correspond to social moves they are making, the pencil fixing the social gesture at each turn.

One afternoon, for example, during an outer space unit, Amy (3:9) tipped over the big windowed box the group had made into a walk-in spaceship. She cried and, after the episode was resolved, sat down by herself in another part of the room. Dinah (also 3:9) came over to her and began to draw pictures for her. Next, Dinah asked me how to spell "sick" and "I hope you feel better." As I dictated the letters, she wrote them on another piece of paper. She accessorized her words with small drawings of raindrops and clouds, other elements of gray sadness that, like sickness, make you feel bad (Britsch, 1992).

Dinah took this composition to Amy and added to it this oral reading: "It says, 'I hope you feel . . . better' and raindrops and rain clouds. Amy, you can *keep* it."

Amy took the card, but held it upside down.

"It goes this way," Dinah explained kindly and turned it

Introducing New Genres

As astute observers, teachers take their cues from children's activity. It's often the children who introduce new and interesting genres. To expand on such an interest, teachers can briefly introduce different conventional genres to the children during whole-group time: letters, notes, or recipes, for example. Read excerpts from cookbooks, science journals, and other grown-up sources with the children. As you read, ask the children to tell you why the example is set up as it is based on its purpose—for instance, why recipes list the ingredients first and then give the instructions (e.g., Green, 1992). Use appropriate terminology, such as "procedure" for a science report, so that these become natural parts of the experience for the children. The genres should correspond with the functions you see in the children's play and the types of writing that the children have been noticing or commenting about. To tailor these presentations to the children's own experience, cognition, and play, link a familiar purpose with a new form, or vice versa: use notes for a new purpose, for example. Model the process and then see what the children do: "Here's another way." Or "This is how scientists might do it."

Then, during a lengthy (at least 45 minutes) small-group or center time, let the children take over in transforming these genres in their own play scenes, infusing the new genres with their own social purposes. This kind of composing need not be limited to a specific time during the day. To link function with form, new purposes should provoke new genre forms throughout the day as new scenes arise in everyday activity.

---

around. "Yeah," she went on, "see all those raindrops . . . between all the um—between all the letters?"

"Mmhm," Amy acknowledged offhandedly.

"You can take them home and hang them—and hang those on your *wall* for—if you're sick you'll always have those pictures. And when you grow *up*, you can wait till you have little *kids* and give those pictures to *your* little kids . . . I was sick before too—" she began to explain, almost giving Amy a set of instructions for the use of the get-well card.

Here, Dinah used the genre of the get-well card as part of her response to an emotional event. Her composing combined drawing, written language, and explanation, all toward the social end of caregiving. Amy, for her part, understood that written words

Figure 2.4 Dinah's "get well" card.

carry a message, but accepted Dinah's social gesture in much the same way that one accepts the gift of a candy dish meant as an ashtray.

"'Kay," Amy interrupted. "I'mon tell you a story! Once upon a time," Amy began to read from Dinah's card, "there was—can you see it?"

With this teacher language, Amy cast Dinah in the subordinate role.

Stumped, Dinah answered resignedly, "You—I'll—I—well . . . I'll make a story." She began to write in her "cursive" style on another sheet of paper (Britsch, 1992).

Amy, get-well card still in hand, began again: "Once upon a time—"

At this, Dinah gave up and stopped writing. "*That's* just the

Figure 2.5 Dinah's cursive story.

picture," she explained. "That's just a PICTURE!"

"Once upon a time—can I read this to you?" Amy persisted.

"It's just a DECORATION with WORDS!" Dinah explained, exasperated.

In response, Amy put down the card and picked up one of the child-dictated books from the classroom bookshelf. "Can I read this to you?" she asked sweetly.

"Yes." Dinah gave in.

Amy "read" the story by singing her own words to it, and then suggested, "Know what, Dinah? You can take this home to you—you can take this home . . . if you want to."

Dinah had meant to soothe the tipping-over incident with the get-well card, but Amy took control of the whole scene by simply changing the genre. It was a case of dueling compositions: one fiction and the other nonfiction. Dinah actually made social use of two nonfiction genres here, one oral (her explanation or instructions to Amy about how to use the card) and one written (the get-well card itself). All of this composing play emerged from the maternal stance Dinah had taken toward Amy (physically smaller but the same age), and from the interaction between two personalities as they encountered each other.

Assessing What Children Know about Genres Other than Stories

If children's responses to scenes like these are the beginnings of nonfiction literacy, what do children know about genre? How do they conceive of it? How can we find out? We can distinguish the graphic forms of children's composing products, the oral genres that accompany these forms, and the social functions of these genres in classroom scenes. We might document these systematically by assembling a chart of the type illustrated in table 2.1.

We can learn many things from such a chart. For instance, one of the most important literacy functions for Dinah was caring for others. This meshed with her personality, and will provide further insights as time goes on. We can also see that from the ages of three years, nine months, to three years, eleven months, Dinah moved from longer dictated messages to the one-word designations that she sounded out and wrote on her own. At the same time Laura, at four years, three months, was just beginning to work on alphabet letters as first order symbols and did not necessarily understand that speech can be "drawn" (although, in another context or scene she might show just such an understanding). Josh, at four years, three months, was using linear mock writing to convey lengthy messages for varied social purposes. He used literacy in sophisticated ways: both his letter to Millie and his estimates expressed his desire to be included with others. Socially, he was testing just these waters at that time, and he enlisted writing to help him. We can also see that more than one child engaged in the use of explanation as an oral genre (like Sam in Chapter 1). Another common oral genre was the announcement or warn-

Table 2.1 Elements of Some Nonfiction Compositions

CHILD (AGE)	MEDIUM: GRAPHIC	MEDIUM: ORAL	SOCIAL GESTURE
Jason (2:9)	Drawing of flying airplane	Label; designate	Convey impression of flight
Dinah (3:9)	Drawn and written card	Read print message, explain uses for the card	Console, provide caregiving, explain/instruct
Dinah (3:11)	Written prescription	Carry out an act appropriate to a dramatized scene, reinforced by physical gesture (taping prescription to patient)	Provide remedy, caregiving
Darrin (3:11)	Written/drawn newspaper	Announce	Enforce power domain
Group of girls (3:7 to 4:3)	Linear mock signs (Post-its)	Warn	Include/exclude
Josh (3:9)	Linear mock estimates	Small talk to propel giving and getting of estimates	Include self with others, dramatize a real-world purpose using non-narrative composing
Josh (4:3)	Linear mock letter	Read letter aloud	Invite, express emotion of missing someone
Laura (4:3)	First order symbol: "S"	Explain	Give gift

ing as a statement of power. This, too, coincides developmentally with the power struggle of the four-year-old year.

A range of conventional and child-created genres pop up very early in the composing of children. Newkirk has pointed out how adeptly children can use genres other than stories. "Anyone who has ever argued with a three-year-old," he states, "knows that children are not limited to stories, that when provoked they seem to bring the universe of discourse to bear on recalcitrant parents" (Newkirk, 1985, p. 595). In fact, according to Bissex's work (as cited in Newkirk, 1985), children's self-created signs may contain the elements of argument. The first sign, below, requests a kind of behavior accompanied by a reason for this request:

> DO NAT DSTRB GNYS AT WRK
> Do not disturb. Genius at work (Bissex, 1980, as cited in Newkirk, 1985, p. 597).

In a subsequent sign, Newkirk points out that the same child writer uses his second statement to amend, or qualify, his demand:

> DO.NAT KM.IN.ANE.MOR.JST.LETL.KES
> Do not come in anymore. Just little kids (Bissex, 1980, as cited in Newkirk, 1985, p. 597).

These signs make a social gesture slightly more elaborate than the "party" signs and newspaper of the preschoolers described earlier. In both, though, we start with situations that provoke social gestures made through literacy—not the other way around.

"Any models," Newkirk warned, "which suggest that beginning writers are limited to a single kind of discourse fail to account for the diversity, even the virtuosity, of the beginning writer" (1985, p. 602). Some children may deem nonfiction composition more useful than stories, particularly in differing kinds of situations, or they may do so for a while. If we make room for different kinds of scenes in the classroom and vary the genres we assess, we may uncover a vast new repertoire of genre knowledge for many children in the group.

Children also demonstrate their knowledge about literacy through readings of their own work. Liliana Barro Zecker (1999) studied the final products of a group of kindergartners and first-graders who were asked to write three kinds of texts at three different times during one school year: a story, a shopping list, and a letter to a friend. She found that children's readings of their own products were crucial. Although the children used emergent writing forms, they knew a lot about the specific characteristics of a given genre. This knowledge emerged as they read their texts back to the researchers after composing them.

Zecker also found that the list was the best-known genre to

the children in contrast with their knowledge about the content and style of letters and stories. At first, many children did not really write "stories" but informational pieces such as "all about" texts actually composed of a series of facts. These were not stories at all. Some children mixed factual genres with the formulaic openings and closings of stories. Letters were often turned into stories, suggesting that some children may not know how to use written language for anything other than a fictional narrative. In fact, if children are exposed primarily to pattern books, this may be the type of product they are most likely to create—appropriately or inappropriately—in response to a situation that requires a piece of writing.

Like Vygotsky (1978), Newkirk reminds us that "there is no fixed path" along which this kind of literacy development proceeds (1985, p. 602). Most essential, however, is the point that children begin with and must retain a voice in this development. This

Observation as Assessment

By creating varied contexts for children's nonfiction composing as well as for story creation, teachers can document (a) growth in composers' control of narrative and non-narrative genres, (b) the mixture of talk, drawing, and writing that children use for various composing purposes, and (c) the differential strengths of composers. Teachers can create multigenre portraits of literacy development beginning with a composing activity involving a single child.

Proceed as follows: Provide materials that you select (e.g., blank paper, lined paper, large paper, a booklet of paper, markers, pencils, crayons). Ask the child, in whatever way you wish, to make two kinds of texts as did Zecker (1999); for example, try a story and a list, or a poem and a letter. See if you can use one imaginative and one factual genre. Record what the child does and says while composing the text, and (optionally) audiotape the event. Photocopy any graphic products you obtain during this observation and include them in your assessment. Share your results with parents; the range of knowledge children demonstrate at school and at home may differ or may mirror each other. Your explanations about the children's products and their readings will help parents to appreciate what their children are doing. In turn, parents will be able to provide you with insights into the child's literacy activities away from school.

kind of voice gives the child writer considerable power and control, control that is central to participation in written discourse (Gee, 1987). Why remove this by asking children to write in contexts that *we* associate with children's culture—whether the children do or not? Why are descriptions of "The Time I Threw Up" so much more compelling than the labored churnings of "My Summer Vacation"? Why do so many students view writing in the same way that I, unfortunately, once viewed algebra: useful for what? As teachers, we can use the information we have about the conventions of genre to guide children in trying new ways of representing their knowledge. These conventions are the focus of the next chapter.

Chapter 3

Composing Choices

Representing Response to Experience

Response as Choice

Genres are more than the forms they take. We also distinguish them by the things they do because genres are social gestures. In other words, we compose in order to do something in the world (Kress, 1993). Nonfiction compositions (oral, drawn, and written) are ways of acting, or responding, to situations; as such they rarely have one single social purpose or "one definable social meaning" (Cope and Kalantzis, 1993, p. 16). In fact, the nonfiction composing of young children may best be described as "antigenre," a kind of reinvention that matches a social purpose with a new set of forms or conventions for conveying that response (Peters, 1997, p. 201). This means that children's nonfiction composing may accomplish a variety of social purposes by using an amalgam of what we would recognize as conventional, or standard, literary genres.

Children show different perspectives on experience through their composing, using a repertoire of strategies to do this, as we saw in Chapters 1 and 2. They develop into independent and resourceful adult composers by being able to make choices about genre (Wiley, 2000) as informed by those already available in the language. This enables composers to actively participate in the conversations in various fields, to make appropriate communicative choices in different situations, and to handle the responses that come back.

This chapter will first examine nonfiction as both a narrative and non-narrative choice in order to provide some background about conventional composing choices and frequently used terms. Next, it presents a collection of some of the composing choices of child composers, as well as some ideas about what teachers can do in response. This involves asking what the child was using the piece to do, what the child saw as most central in the context, and how the chosen form or structure mirrored that function. The answers to these questions then drive teaching.

Where Does Nonfiction Fit?

Narrative composition is not always fictional. Much narrative, composition that chronicles or tells a story, is nonfiction. On the other hand, some exposition is non-narrative: description, argument, analysis. Not all nonfiction is non-narrative. This chapter will first focus on the differences between narrative and non-narrative, looking at the ways in which fiction and nonfiction fit with these categories.

What Is Narrative?

Narrative is quite often equated with fiction. Narrative tells what happened, it sequences events (Decker and Schwegler, 1992). Of course, narrative text—written or oral—can convey a sequence of imaginative events. But much narrative is nonfictional in nature. Biography and autobiography are examples of narrative writing that tells true stories. In classrooms, narrative (equated with "fiction") is too often signaled by the clichéd opening "Once upon a time." Narrative does allow composers to tell stories that aren't happening in this very moment, stories that are distant from us in time (Toolan, 1988, p. 2). But a narrative account may also chronicle the history of a science investigation, for example. In a sense, mathematical equations are a kind of narration because they describe behaviors and chronicle the relationships between them.

Both fiction and nonfiction are different ways of "doing narrative." They overlap each other and can fulfill many of the same purposes. Fiction and nonfiction can both serve composers as frames for picturing their lives. The composer decides which events, emotional or physical, to recount and which aspects of those events will play a role or be discounted in the sense-making process. Jerome Bruner has said that our ways of telling and conceptualizing our stories become so habitual that our stories about ourselves turn into recipes for structuring experience itself. Our stories not only guide our life narratives up to the present but direct it into the future. "A life," Bruner argues, "is not 'how it was' but how it is interpreted and reinterpreted, told and retold" (1988, p. 582). All of us carry with us an interior narrative, or history, that helps us to integrate what happens to us into the story of who we are and how we understand things.

This is what children do with their composing, given the chance. Eric's leaf composition in Chapter 1 interpreted his idea of "change" narratively. The drawings in Deanna's street montage did not explicitly sequence events in this way, but her talk linked relevant visual elements through explanation and description. This wasn't as much narrative as it was exposition. Each composer, however, was interpreting experience through both narrative and non-narrative tools.

Narrative, either real or imaginary, usually shows intention as well as action, the accidents and consequences of being human (Bruner, 1986). It explores what people know, think, and feel. In fact, fictional narrative can communicate more truth than nonfiction. How? A novelist can illustrate motives, moods, reasons, and circumstances that an interview subject may not wish to reveal or recall. A journalist who attempts to portray a life may be limited not only by boundaries of privacy, but also by a reluctance to probe and reveal certain details (Benedict, 1999). In the same way, the elements of fiction help some children to explain concepts that seem distant, but these should not remain the only tools available to them. If so, children may see an informational piece comprising a series of facts as a "story" (Zecker, 1999). Older students may continue the habit of reporting information gained from a text narratively (Collins, as cited in Wiley, 2000).

What Is Non-Narrative?

Simply stated, a non-narrative text (oral or graphic) doesn't tell a story. There are many conventional non-narrative genres, such as the following:

- labels or signs
- lists
- letters
- classifications
- procedures or instructions
- descriptions
- explanations
- analyses
- arguments
- information reports

The boundaries blend. For example, while letters can be classified as a non-narrative genre, they may also tell someone's story. Through other eyes, a letter may not be seen as a genre at all, but as "a medium for a number of different genres," such as recounts, reports, descriptions, or sets of directions (Derewianka, 1990, p. 76).

What Is Exposition?

Exposition is sometimes equated with "non-narrative" text. Most essentially, expository writing "exposes" and shares information (Decker and Schwegler, 1992) as its primary purpose. It may also employ narrative as a device to clarify its description or explanation. The main purpose of expository text, however, is not to convey the writer's feelings about the topic, to argue, or to tell a story. If a composer examines Internet usage and then characterizes it as a cultural phenomenon, it's still expository even though it also contains the writer's views. In this sense, persuasive writing, such as a newspaper editorial, is not expository. Some arguments, however, employ expository techniques (e.g., describing or elaborating). An essay wouldn't be considered expository, because its primary purpose is to offer the author's personal impression or opinion, although this is opinion informed by fact. Varying definitions of "exposition" exist in the literature, however. Another view (see, for instance, Derewianka, 1990; Green, 1992; Martin, 1993) characterizes exposition as a genre in which the writer takes a stand on an issue. An expository piece contains a judgment (or thesis) and addresses the social significance of the issue, beyond just explaining it.

Children may use drawn, written, oral, and dictated exposition in order to pull an unfamiliar external context (a new context that came from without) toward a more familiar, internalized context (a context they already understand). As composers, they bring the scenes that are the most salient—most important and immediate for them—into the context of talk with others and onto the context of the page. This combines fact with significant personal experience through which children become interpreters of significant changes in their lives.

Newkirk (1989) argues that expository competence develops as students build upon early non-narrative genres such as labeling (e.g., signs) and list making. Later, more integrated forms of exposition develop, such as description or explanation. Moffett contends, however, that exposition develops from narrative competence because writers learn to generalize from "what happened" to "what happens (1965, p. 45)." Moffett also argues, however, that children cannot generalize at length and do not embed lower-level abstraction in the higher-level abstraction in the general-to-specific order required by true exposition (Newkirk, 1989). In the collection of composing choices that follows, exposition as explanation and description sometimes employs narrative and often includes generalization (as did Eric and Sam in Chapter 1).

The view undergirding this book is that the development of all genres is not a normative process but that it emerges from the need, intent, and desire of composers. It is also highly reliant on the understanding shown by the audience, usually the teacher, of the complexity and detail in the children's composing. What's clear is that children use a variety of genres in varying emergent forms to do things in their world. Not all children may be concerned to produce a story, so their composing should not be evaluated for its quality as a "story." Teachers can learn a great deal about the understandings a child is constructing through their observation of children's composing choices. Teachers can also learn about the mechanisms that are familiar and unfamiliar to a composer and how these are working for that individual.

Why focus on all of this detail? If complexity in composing choices beyond stories is a goal, teachers need information about what they're teaching so they can broaden the options for child composers. The genre categories teachers recognize also promote certain values; for example, is Deanna's montage acceptable? How about Eric's leaf narrative? Or Sam's explanation of photosynthesis? Teachers have the power to decide and to question:

♦ What kinds of composing will we encourage?
♦ What will we discourage or praise?
♦ What will we counsel children to revise and "improve" the composition?
♦ How will we guide child composers?
♦ How will we encourage the representation of experience in individual ways, but ways that will be seen as trustworthy and valuable by readers?

A Collection of Composing Choices

Introducing children to new composing choices involves helping them to represent their relationships to situations by organizing what they know, learn, and perceive (Kress, 1994). Table 3.1 summarizes some possible composing choices along with a few of the elements that characterize each one. Just as this collection does not represent every possible choice, each set of elements should be seen as an option and not as a compulsory ingredient for a successful composition.

This collection juxtaposes and combines child-created composing choices with conventional genres. The composing choices are not mutually exclusive; that is, one may incorporate another, using it as a device to accomplish its own central purpose. No normative sequence is implied here. The purpose of this collection is to illustrate the range and depth of functioning shown in children's work and a way of looking at some of the conventions to which this functioning is related. Informed both by convention and by the child, teachers can truly notice what child composers are trying to show them.

As teachers, we need to be careful not to reduce our teaching to a normative set of templates or forms that we simply transmit to children. Instead, we can use what we know about conventional, or standard, choices to heighten our awareness of the kinds of choices that are available to children, given a context. Here's where we may offer additional experience, a new connection provoking a next response and the need for new composing choices. Over

Table 3.1. Some Nonfiction Composition Choices

COMPOSING CHOICE	WHAT IT DOES	FEATURES
Object description/ concept list	Provides a set of most salient details, or a logically organized list of concepts, about someone or something: "How I Saw Something."	◆ Represents details as they are arranged in space ◆ Observer stays in a single spot or may move ◆ May evoke emotion or remain impartial ◆ Expresses relevant detail ◆ Uses precise vocabulary ◆ May list concepts or ideas in sentences
Activity description	Chronicles personal activity of the composer (narrator) in a particular situation: "How I Did Something."	◆ Personal activity in a single situation is sequentially organized ◆ Focuses on narrator as participant ◆ First-person pronouns ◆ Temporal connectors ◆ Limited length ◆ Immediate time frame
How explanation	Chronicles a generalized process, not through a description of personal action but objectively: "How Something Happens" or "How Something Works."	◆ Statement of goal ◆ List of the materials ◆ Steps of the process in order
Why explanation	Explains observed phenomena through cause-and-effect reasoning.	◆ Identifies the phenomenon ◆ Identifies cause and effect
Classification	Sorts and patterns objects, phenomena and results.	◆ Organizing statement/thesis ◆ Definition/description of each category, or set of information ◆ Organized in a logical progression

continued

Table 3.1. *(continued)*

Argument	States an opinion or presents a position based on facts in order to persuade the reader to accept this position.	• Claim • Evidence (fact) • Recommendation(s)
Nonfiction narrative/recount	Recounts past activity of self or others narratively; may unite several events over time; communicates the sense that the composer has made of the events, not simply a series of steps toward a result.	• Orientation • Logical ordering of several events or situations • Past tense, active verbs • Varied use of connectives • First person for personal recounts • Third person to recount others' experience • Precise and vivid word choices • Contains details of setting and action that the composer can see but the listener can't • May contain dialogue
Research report	Presents an informational investigation or experiment carried out by the composer.	• Aim or research questions • Method/procedure • Facts organized into paragraphs in logical order, revealing patterns or different aspects of the topic • Results reveal patterns observed by the composer in the investigation • Data tables, charts, or diagrams may summarize results • Conclusions draw meaning from results • Conclusions, which may include *why* explanation

time, we would hope for more complexly organized structures, but what is complexity at any particular developmental moment for any particular child? First, we need to recognize the different ways in which children are using language and images to accomplish a variety of social purposes. The next sections will explore several composing choices through classroom scenes, examining how children respond to different situations and how teachers might work with these composing choices as ways of representing responses to experience. Unlike those in Chapter 2, these representations are accomplished primarily through drawing and conventional written symbols.

Object and Activity Description/ Concept Lists

Description, a non-narrative device, provides details about what something or someone is like. Description is not always seen as a genre in and of itself, but is often viewed as a support for narrative, process analysis, argument and other genres. Description can add precise vocabulary and sensory or emotional detail to develop a point being made (Dietsch, 2000). In early childhood classrooms, for example, children are often asked to tell or write about a picture. This results in description rather than "stories" because the visual context suggests detailing a static scene or an object that is depicted. Nothing suggests a narrative—dynamic movement or dramatic action (Hough, Nurss, and Wood, 1987). Young children do use drawing, talk, and writing to describe in more than one way, however.

Object Description

Object descriptions usually present details as they would be seen or arranged in space (Decker and Schwegler, 1992). The observer might stay in a single spot, like a photographer, or move from one position to another (Dietsch, 2000). Some descriptions are written to evoke an emotional response from the reader; others are impartial and factual. In either, the use of detail expressed through very precise and vivid vocabulary choice is essential to presenting a mental picture through language.

Grammatically, object descriptions can also comprise lists of sentences. Cognitively, these may also be called concept lists. A teacher can ask, and help the composer to determine, whether the concepts represented through oral language, drawing, and/or writing are logically ordered or random. In this way, concept lists go beyond labeling objects or people and mirror the way in which the composer has linked the ideas at hand.

Activity Description.

Child composers also frequently focus description on their own activity. In activity descriptions, the composer presents an oral, written, and/or drawn chronicle of his or her own activity. Activity descriptions are narrative in the sense that they record a sequence of actions from the point of view of the narrator (the actor), but they also focus on the narrator as a participant. They are categorized here as descriptions because they tend to relate the narrator's immediate and very specific activity, almost as a series of steps. They lack the storylike quality used to recount a visit to the park, for example. Elaborated nonfiction narrative (i.e., recounts) also characterizes experience from the narrator's point of view, but it usually reveals much more about the narrator's experience of the events as remarkable, ridiculous, upsetting, or life-changing. In contrast, activity descriptions simply list the identity of the actions and the order in which they occurred, the bare-bones of what happened.

Scene 1: Describing Objects.

As an emergent science literacy activity, one group of kindergartners used eyedroppers to drip water on Petoskey Stones. In this classroom, the children first made science journal entries showing what they knew about "rocks" in general. Afterwards, they entered what they'd learned. Sophie's first entry, shown in Figure 3.1, was a quite straightforward description of the perceptual information she had about rocks: "The rocks are hard," she wrote. She reiterated the word "hrd" on the right side of her page, further describing the rock she had drawn and indicating it with an arrow.

Another composer, Nicholas, composed a drawing of a scientist, labeled "S," with a cartoon bubble indicating the scientist's words, "A rock." More specifically, Nicholas labeled a Petoskey

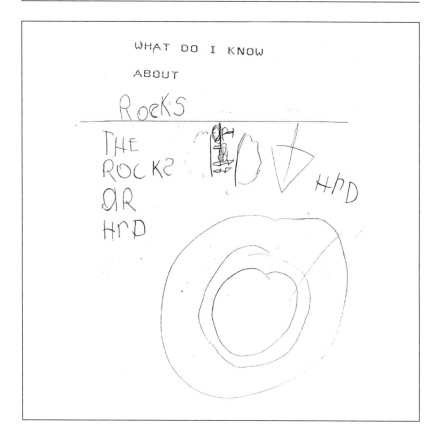

Figure 3.1 Sophie's object-description.

rock beside the scientist with "P." Above the scientist is an accurate drawing of a Petoskey Stone with two hexagons visible on its
surface. Combining both drawing and written language, Nicholas
composed a detailed description of the rock (see Figure 3.2). His
written language labeled the elements of the description.

Scene 2: Describing Personal Activity.

Petoskey Stones are fragments of fossilized colony corals (of
the Hexagonarla genus). They are found on Michigan's Lower
Peninsula. When wet, a Petoskey Stone's surface reveals a hexag-
onal pattern (Petoskey Regional Chamber of Commerce, 2002).

After watching hexagons emerge from the smooth surface of

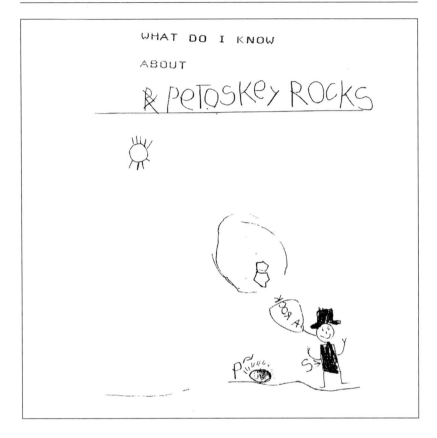

Figure 3.2 Nicholas's object-description.

her stone, Sophie detailed what she saw her second journal entry. She drew the eyedropper and the Petoskey Stone, and wrote: "Wn you pt wtr on the rc" ("When you put water on the rock"). This appears to be merely a sentence fragment, but it actually describes the eyedropper and the state or condition that occurs after water is put on the rock. Sophie also colored the water on the rock. Her drawing and her phrasal label described what she did and what she used to do it, as in Figure 3.3.

Sophie's activity description actually goes beyond a first-person account. She uses the second-person pronoun "you" instead of "I" throughout. Here she's generalizing; she sees that this is not just something that happens to her own Petoskey Stone. Later on, she might show what happens to the stone as a result of putting

Figure 3.3 Sophie's activity-description.

the water on it. This would be the beginning of an explanation. To further analyze the process, she might explain why the water was put on the rock and what the results were. Because Sophie is beginning to generalize, her teacher might now ask "What made it happen?" This is a leading question and could either pull the child further toward an activity-based explanation (e.g., "Because I put water on it") or toward a conventional scientific explanation (e.g., "Water made the hexagons come out").

Nicholas's object description suggests that he is actually less interested in what he did than in the attributes of the Petoskey Stone. Thus, while Sophie's piece describes a process, Nicholas's describes an object (see, for instance, Shepardson and Britsch, 2000). Neither composition, however, contains an explanation for why the hexagons appear. In fact, the water doesn't cause the pattern; it simply makes the pattern more visible, as with tree rings.

It may be tempting to see a story in Nicholas's composition because it seems to contain a character who has probably carried out a series of actions. But the kinds of questions we tend to ask about fictional narratives (i.e., stories) are not those we ask about science: How would you feel if you were the scientist? How would *you* like to end the story? How does the story make you feel? Is there a problem and a resolution? Perhaps, however, we could ask Nicholas to follow the character's scientific activity. This would surely lead to some kind of narrative, probably containing a good deal of description. Still, it would not explain as scientific models do. While writing *by* scientists usually measures, classifies, decomposes, or explains (Martin, 1993), writing *about* scientists is often narrative in nature. Viewing Nicholas's composition as a story would tend to focus him on writing, drawing, or talking about the scientist and what he has done. This suggests another choice: focusing on Nicholas's own center of interest—the rock's appearance and the reasons for it. As with Sophie, this enables us to go from a description of the rock to an activity-based explanation for its current appearance. This both stretches Nicholas's capacities and invites him into the same progression that would engage a scientist—the move from description to explanation.

Scene 3: Combining Object and Activity Description.

The next composition, by a third grader, combines both object description and activity description. As part of a soil project, the class went outdoors to examine what lay underground in several small holes dug in the playground turf. When asked to write about what he'd found, one child composed the following:

> Well we dug a hole into see what was in ther! Then we drew a picture of what we saw. We wer in groups of four. We mostly saw catipillers. They were very long. One boy in are group did not like them. It was fun.

This composition begins with a description of the children's activity: in groups of four, they dug holes and drew pictures. It continues with a series of short descriptions that list the children's findings: "We mostly saw catipillers. They were very long." The composition concludes with some personal commentary by the writer indicating that one student didn't like the creatures that were found.

What is paramount here for both teacher and student is to clarify the student's understandings about the described observations. By noting that the composition is primarily descriptive, a teacher might talk with the student to address its factual inaccuracy. Why would caterpillars be found underground? For what reasons would they not be found there? Providing the answers to these questions would involve more description—of the environments where caterpillars are found, the conditions under which they survive, the environments and needs of earthworms, centipedes, millipedes, or whatever the child observed. This time, though, the description would work toward an explanation for the findings the student has made, and then toward revision. The revision itself might explain why the student changed his mind, a result of comparing information about caterpillars and earthworms. An error can enable a student to stretch from description to explanation.

Explanations

Explanations do more than simply tell what happened, they tell why, or try to tell why. Young children generally explain logically but often unconventionally, based on what they know and have experienced, not on adult logic and factual awareness. For children's explanations, we will distinguish two composing choices: *why* explanations and *how* explanations.

Why Explanation

In conventional terms, *why* explanations generally address cause-and-effect relationships, as did Sam's attempt at explaining plant growth in Chapter 1. Structurally, these usually begin by identifying the phenomenon in question and they continue with the explanation itself (Derewianka, 1990). Alternatively, they may present a cause, or causes, and then the effect(s) (Dietsch, 2000).

In contrast, *how* explanations analyze processes or show the way toward a result (Dietsch, 2000). Formally, they present the steps of the process in order, often beginning with some statement of the goal, a list or description of the materials, and then the method (Derewianka, 1990). Here are some illustrations.

Scene 4: Explaining Why.

After a leaf walk near the school, one kindergartner responded by drawing a leaf, which she colored green and outlined in brown on one side. She wrote, "There are brown leaves. The green of the leaves peel off." (See Figure 3.4.)

This child composer began her piece with the *effect* portion of the cause-and-effect relationship she is attempting to explain: "The leaves are brown." To reverse it, here is the cause: the green part of the leaves peels off. She has created a *why* explanation for the pigment change. It is unconventional but logically based on the child's own experiences with color change.

Older children also attempt *why* explanations that may be equally unconventional. One third grader offered the following

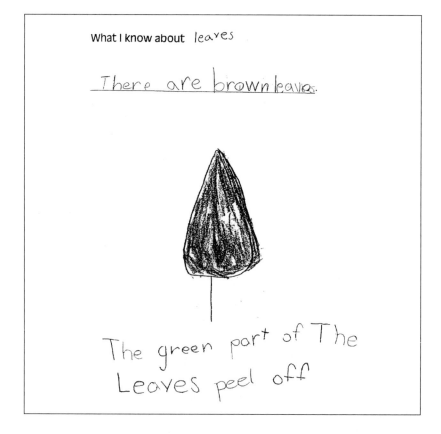

What I know about leaves

There are brown leaves.

The green part of The Leaves peel off

Figure 3.4 A kindergartener's *why*-explanation.

explanation for pigment change after examining a set of decayed leaves:

> I will tell you why the leaves change color. In the spring time leaves our fine. But when the heat gets colder the sugar goes away and it doesn't make food anymore. Red, yellow, or orange might show up when the chlorophyll goes away.

This composer identified the phenomenon and provided an accurate explanation for it. This piece of exposition makes use of narration to trace a long-term process, and is also clearly addressing an audience: "you." This structures the composing choice: the author needs to begin by focusing her reader's thinking on a topic. the writer does this by indicating her social intent: she's going to respond to a question that was asked. Although this composer's response might have included research using an external source, she's represented the concepts in her own voice—not a copied one. The audience provides a frame for her response; in fact, it was sent as an e-mail so the audience is a real one. These kinds of writing opportunities alter the classroom notion that the audience is the teacher, and give children the power to choose and tailor a response.

Another composer explained the same phenomenon in a highly perceptual way:

> I think when the leaves change color because they fal of and then thear is dye in the tree and then the dye drops on the leave changes color.

This composer also identified the phenomenon and provided an explanation. The "dye in the tree" is not far removed from the idea of pigment. Perhaps a teacher response to this composition could introduce the technical term "*pigment,*" which does fade as chlorophyll breaks down. This might make a link with something the child has stated before revisiting the phenomenon itself and the reasons for it.

Another issue, however, is that *why* explanations are not always appropriate composing choices for all of the children in a classroom. The situations that are meant to motivate these explanations do not always illustrate phenomena children can comprehend, as in the next example.

Scene 5: Explaining Why.

In one kindergarten, the children explored the classroom with magnets to test for attraction versus non-attraction. The teacher then asked them to record what they had learned about magnets in their science journals. Some of the children drew the objects around the room that did and did not attract the magnet; others recorded the number of objects that did and did not attract. For some children, however, the most fascinating element of the situation was the reason *why* the magnet attracted. One composer, for example, created a non-narrative composition incorporating drawing, invented spelling, and talk (Figure 3.5).

This composer drew magnets in his composition and labeled the strokes around each magnet with "A" to make an invisible force visible through drawing and writing: "A" for "air pressure."

Figure 3.5 A *why*-explanation: air pressure.

According to this logic, it was this force that caused the magnets to attract. This reasoning addressed the cause-and-effect relationships between magnets and substances, resulting in a composition that is primarily a *why* explanation. It also sounded very scientific, and other children soon began to repeat the "air pressure" explanation, including it in their science journals (Britsch, 2001b). To provide a needed conflict, the teacher placed the magnet on the underside of the aluminum chalk tray. When the magnet fell off, she asked why. One child replied, "Because the wind isn't blowing that way." This analysis was consistent with the children's logic.

Can kindergartners really explain magnetic attraction? Perhaps this apparently very concrete subject matter does not lend itself to much in-depth explanation by young children. A kindergartner will certainly not understand the molecular explanation for magnetic attraction. A more appropriate aim, however, may be for the child to identify the items that attract and those that do not, concluding that not all objects attract. Such a response can be represented through a non-narrative composing choice: a classification. This could become quite complex and descriptive if, for example, the classification distinguished the attributes of those items that do attract from the attributes of those that don't. This would reveal the fact that physical characteristics, such as shininess, do not predict magnetic attraction. This begins the idea that some other factor is involved, or that some metals do attract, but not all. Alternatively, this whole process could be documented through a research report that traces the children's hypotheses (e.g., silver objects, metallic objects, shiny objects), their tests, and their results (see "Research Reports," below).

How Explanation

Children may also convey what they understand through another kind of explanation: a *how* explanation. *How* explanations, sometimes called process analyses, tell how something is done (Dietsch, 2000)—for instance, how to make cookies, how something works, how to reach a goal, or how a state or condition evolves. *How* explanations can be seen as a kind of narration (Decker and Schwegler, 1992). They often have a narrative quality; but they really don't aim to tell a story in the way that narratives do. Their purpose is to characterize a generalized process.

In contrast, narratives usually aim to show something about human intention, to explore what the participants know, think, and feel (Bruner, 1986, p. 13). *How* explanations, or process analyses, focus on the how-to aspect of a sequence of events. In this way, they take a step toward sustained generalization for child composers.

It is important to distinguish *how* explanations from both activity descriptions and *why* explanations. A child who, for example, pours a mixture of sand and pebbles through a sieve might compose an oral activity description like this one:

> I poured the mixture and the sand fell to the bottom and the pebbles were at the top.

Or the child might create a *how* explanation for what happened:

> The sieve traps the pebbles and lets the sand fall through.

In contrast, a *why* explanation for the same phenomenon would indicate that this occurred because the particle size of the pebbles was larger than the holes in the sieve (Shepardson and Britsch, 2000).

Both activity descriptions and *how* explanations employ narration, but the primary purpose of a *how* explanation is to characterize a generalized procedure (e.g., how a sieve traps pebbles). This is related to the *why* of that particular phenomenon—the *why* explains the *how*. In a *how* explanation, the *why* is not stated. *How* explanations might be seen as more abstract than activity descriptions because they generalize; they take another step back from one's own immediate activity. In this sense, they can be seen as reflections on, rather than representations of, a series of actions.

We can also differentiate *how* explanations from object descriptions. For example, a composer may draw the kernels of corn and the mortar and pestle used to grind corn. This is a visual object description that may underlie a *how* explanation of the grinding process that employs these implements. Description can be necessary to explanation, but description alone does not explain.

Scene 6: Explaining How.

Eric's leaf composition in Chapter 1 visually described and verbally traced how a process evolved, although it didn't explain why that process took place:

The leaf is falling . . . falling . . . falling. When it gets to the bottom, it shows leaf veins. Then . . . compost.

As a kindergartner, Eric would not necessarily derive the scientific *why* explanation for pigment change or leaf decay, but he certainly ordered some of the steps. Still, his composition was not primarily a storylike kind of narrative; it did represent his understanding, but it also attempted a kind of explanation—telling not why but how leaves decay. Neither did it describe how *he* did something. This means that, in terms of expository text, we can differentiate children's descriptions of how *they* did something from descriptions of how something *is* done.

Scene 7: Explaining Why.

The italicized portion of the following composition by a third grader explains how boa constrictors trap their prey:

> The boa can stay in a tree for 12 hours *when it sees its pray it will drop down from the tree and squeese its pray.* the boa is one of the largest snakes in the world.

The other two statements in the composition are object descriptions, facts about boa constrictors. They frame the composition at beginning and end, but they sound as if they are not in the child's voice. They stand out from what really seems to interest this composer the most. When the voice changes, active verbs like *see, drop,* and *squeeze* animate the *how* explanation. In this way, the details of children's composing reflect whose response it really is. Simply asking the composer to talk about the part of the boa's behavior that interests him the most may open up new questions, and the need for new and more complex explanations. By thinking through this reasoning process with the child, we provide a kind of cognitive modeling that will enable the child to think in new and possibly unfamiliar ways.

The next composition also appears to begin by explaining how boa constrictors trap their prey.

> The boa hids in trees when it sees it's pray it drops down and raps around it's pray and gives it a big squese. Then it eats his food head first. *He eat his food heads first because if he ate tail first he would choke on the head.* The boa can squese on alagater but it would take a few days to eat.

This composer, however, interjects the italicized *why* explanation for one of the snake's behaviors when consuming its prey, signaled by the connective "because." When this composer turns to alligators, he's got the beginning of a new theme—a paragraph—that could lead to decomposing the elements of the boa constrictor's diet and the process of ingestion for each. There are many directions to take. The ideas are there for this composer, but the trick is to keep to the primary phenomenon he's trying to explain. It's just that he hasn't explicitly identified this at the beginning of the piece. Stating the unstated may, in this case, guide the composer's further choices about information and organization. To do this, teachers can help children to revisit their own responses and pull out contradictions, conflicting purposes, and the ways in which composing choices are working to accomplish the composer's aims. This fosters the ability to make choices that direct independent composing.

Teachers need to recognize whether the child is explaining how or explaining why. Children may not always begin with *how* explanations, and there's no normative progression from *how* to *why*. It's simply the case that some issues interest a child and others don't. Very young children may not be developmentally ready to understand the elements of some explanations; they may only be able to repeat back. In this case, the composing is not based in the child's reality but in the teacher's. Because it does not address the contexts that the children bring to the task, this composing does not reflect the connections that children are making for themselves.

Classification

All language is classification, and children are constantly classifying the world through their language use (Jones, 1986). They are searching for patterns and regularities in the world. In fact, classification also mirrors the way at least one area of inquiry organizes the universe: science. Science writing classifies, measures, decomposes, and explains (Martin, 1993). It doesn't tell stories, although, behind a non-narrative representation lies the narrative of the investigation itself—the process leading to the non-narrative product. We can even see equations and formulae as narratives, telling the story of mathematical behaviors. Science is not the only subject area that employs classification as a way of "organizing reality" (Martin, 1993, p. 169). Much explanatory writing uses classification to clarify points, to order information, to set out categories or reasons (Dietsch, 2000). Narratives, too, may use classification for many of these same reasons although classification is not the primary purpose of a narrative.

Classifications, as non-narrative texts, sort and pattern objects, phenomena, and results. Formally, written classifications begin with some general organizing statement, or thesis, about the set of items to be classified. A thesis can simply introduce the topic, or it can suggest the "order of presentation" or an "attitude" toward the topic (Dietsch, 2000, p. 190). Then each category, or logical set of facts, is defined and briefly described (Derewianka, 1990). Classifications usually organize things into a kind of progression—the reasons for some behavior may be classified from simple to complex, for example (Dietsch, 2000).

Children may represent their classifications through drawing (see Chapter 4), through oral language, or both. Like explanations, the classifications of young children usually follow their own experientially based logic and may be very unconventional. Though they are empirically logical, they may still be inaccurate. The objects and activity we provide in the classroom are critical to the formation of children's logical connections. It's these connections that composers mirror in their oral, drawn, and written classifications.

Scene 8: Classifying Crystals.

One group of five- and six-year-olds passed around a geode as they discussed what they knew about rocks. The teacher talked about crystals and the children handled some of these. When the children drew and wrote about what they knew, Nicholas classified the rocks (actually crystals) according to ease of breakability (see Figure 3.6). On the left side of his page he drew a diamond and labeled it with a "D." He also listed its attributes: "S" for "shiny," "VH" for "very hard." Then, above the diamond, he drew a clenched fist at the end of a wrist. Could a fist break a diamond? "ON," he answered in mirror writing (i.e., "NO").

At the top right of his page, Nicholas drew a faceted crystal, which he labeled "C." A chisel, pointed down at the crystal, lined up with a dotted line scoring where the break would be (Britsch, 2001b, p. 114). Nicholas was classifying through labeled diagrams:

WHAT HAVE I LEARNED

ABOUT

Rocks

Figure 3.6 A classification.

some crystals break and others don't. Using word-initial consonants, his diagrams also describe the characteristics of a diamond,
a crystal that does not break easily. Essentially, he tried to explain
by classifying the attributes he observed. A kindergartner is
unlikely to understand that some substances have very strong
bonds between the carbon atoms so that they are harder to pull
apart. Nicholas's classification, however, is based on two conventional properties of crystals: hardness and luster. Nicholas
might now go on with other tests to help him sort these minerals
(e.g., a scratch test, a streak test, an acid test using vinegar).

This composer further contextualized the "rock" theme (a
slight misuse of terminology) using a Flintstones motif. At the bot-

tom right of the page, he drew the closing-time whistle from the quarry where Fred Flintstone worked. Even this related to the criterion that guided this child's classification: Fred Flintstone broke rocks at his job, of course!

Argument

Language that aims to persuade is rhetorical. As such, arguments (a) make their claim, (b) provide evidence, and (c) conclude by either restating the claim or by providing a recommendation to readers or listeners (Derewianka, 1990; Dietsch, 2000). Newspaper editorials, for example, are rhetorical in purpose and form. When the kindergarten teacher in Scene 5 asked the child why the magnet didn't stick to the underside of the chalk tray, the child replied, "Because the wind isn't blowing that way." This is certainly an attempt to explain why, but in the context of this situation it also embodied another kind of response: the oral beginnings of argumentation.

Some allow that expository writing can argue, that it can take a stand on an issue (Green, 1992; Martin, 1993), but the central purpose of exposition is not to provide commentary. For the purposes of this discussion, exposition will be viewed as text that presents facts, describes, and shares information. An expository piece may include commentary that serves its explanation of the importance of an activity or person (Decker and Schwegler, 1992). Effective arguments, however, require a background of fact. In this way, rhetorical pieces make use of exposition, but argumentation most centrally exists to represent the point of view of the author, speaking for him- or herself. It makes an explicit argument (Berne, 2001). It aims to push or pull the reader or listener in one way or another.

Scene 9: Recommending Action.

Charlie, a third grader, was asked what he would tell a friend whose task it was to argue, at a city council meeting, against the construction of a new apartment complex in a wetlands area. Charlie composed the following argument, which also makes use of a bit of explanation:

> One Idea I have is you can tell your freind to tell them that the animals need homes. Just like you need a home. If your

going to build a apartment build It far from the marsh.
Why do you have to build it at the marsh. Maybe they can
have a vote. That is how a lot of people do things. It is fair.
But Before that you should try to talk to congressman. The
hotell will be usfall in all but animals need homes.

How does Charlie argue? He begins by immediately presenting one of his recommendations: "build it far from the marsh."
These usually come at the end of an argument, however, so Charlie
could simply regroup this with his other ideas—voting and talking to a congressman.

There's something else apart from this editing issue: to be persuasive, opinion demands facts. Facts alone do not always persuade, however, and Charlie begins to play on his reader's
emotions by bringing up the fact that animals will be deprived of
their homes if the apartment complex displaces them. He's making an ethical judgment, and also a claim of policy: there are several alternatives that might resolve the issue.

Backing up the composer's personal opinion means research,
either at the library, on the Internet, or by consulting experts on
the subject. Instead of researching first and compiling pages of
information copied at random, Charlie can now be more selective
in what he's looking for. Then he can integrate the information he
needs to back up his views into his composition. His teacher might
ask him how he will argue if his view is challenged. This means
Charlie will need to closely examine and differentiate accurate
from faulty presentations of information. Bringing these kinds of
tools to consciousness gives composers the ability to evaluate and
respond to other situations, to look at alternatives and challenge
assumptions (Whitin and Whitin, 1998). This development takes
time, but it goes far beyond arguments that simply reproduce a
required format using either opinion alone or a set of facts provided by someone else.

Nonfiction Narrative

Narratives report and narratives fictionalize (Moffett, 1968).
In general, nonfiction narratives report or recount the real activity of real people. Unlike activity descriptions, elaborated nonfiction narratives are not limited to recounting the activity of the
composer alone; they can address the experiences of others, too.

They tend to relate events in a storylike way, not as a simple series of steps—as activity descriptions do—and they may extend over a long period of time, uniting many events or situations. In this sense, nonfiction narrative *is* truly narrative: it takes the point of view of the narrator and characterizes the events in question in a particular way. Even the selection of the events to be included communicates a point of view, a slant on the world that already says something about the composer (or narrator) by virtue of the fact that some elements are included and others aren't. A narrative, then, can mean more than it says (Bruner, 1991). Nonfiction narrative interprets the world, makes sense of it, and either values or discounts significant portions of it. In fact, narrative comprehension is among the earliest cognitive abilities to appear in children, a widely used form for organizing one's experience (Bruner, 1991).

Very young children frequently compose this kind of nonfiction narrative through their talk. Ask any child to recall the last time he or she got sick, for example, and you'll elicit a vividly detailed nonfiction narrative that accesses the "sensations, images, feelings and ideas" left behind by that experience and others like it (Rosenblatt, 1988, p. 5). Readers take this kind of "aesthetic stance" (Rosenblatt, 1988, p. 6) , but composing—through telling, drawing, writing, dramatizing—also represents an aesthetic response to experience. Nonfiction narratives communicate this "lived-through meaning" of an event, not the sort of take-away facts we'd expect from a set of directions on a kitchen fire extinguisher (Rosenblatt, 1988, p. 5).

Nonfiction narrative (i.e., recounts) usually orders events chronologically in the past through past-tense verbs. Carefully chosen connectors (such as *first, next, then, after, before*) structure time and order action. Nonfiction narratives can do much more to represent the order of real events, however. They may contain flashbacks, flash-forwards (Bruner, 1991), a switch from past to present-tense verbs, dialogue, action verbs, and lots of relevant visual and concrete details that draw readers into the experience of the narrative through particular eyes. Personal recounts are usually told in first person; as in fictional narrative, the reader gains access to the tale through the teller (Toolan, 1988) so that personal recounts portray events through the eyes of the narrator. Recounts of others' activity are still filtered through the nonfiction narrator but the narrator relates the thoughts and perspectives of the subject, usually (but not always) in third person. The reader then sees as both the author and subject do (Moffett, 1968, p. 136).

Moffett suggests focusing on letters, diaries, and general auto-biography for narrative writing in elementary school because first-person narration does not require the ability to gather the kind of data required for telling what happened to other people (Mottett, 1968, p. 153). Letters (a vanishing genre) and e-mails (often dismissed as ephemeral and insubstantial) lend themselves to recounts in which we sense a great deal of immediacy.

> I went snow skiing again but this time I went down some black dimonds. Im abole to go down the steep stof now. I went on a jump and didn't eevin flyin the air. I went in slush really fast and was trying to take big turns but I did-n't because there was a baby going really slo and by the time she left I was laying down with my head on the ground and my arm spranged and my skeees didn't evin pop off.

This kind of recount goes beyond an activity description. Its pacing, conveyed through descriptions of movement and through its chaining of coordinate clauses, gives it a sense of speed. The tone of the narrative communicates the sense of accidental achievement that the composer took from the experience. This piece is clearly not the result of an assignment to write about summer vacation. Personal recounts enable the composer to sift through events to rediscover them as more or less significant, memorable, cherished, or forgettable. They fix the event as remark-able in the eyes of the composer. In this way, composers become observers of their own lives, they "see the drama of their own lives" (Skenazy, 1998, p. 127). As in fictional narrative, this creates a kind of narrative distance that enables us to make something of what we've done, to see patterns we create, or to explain why— possibly even to ourselves.

> Do you know what happen to my cat? He got attaced by two dogs and died, now I'm relly sad because he was so cute and he had the best personality out of two cats that I've had, but I still have my kitten, but he's not as cute as my cat, his hardliy even cute at all, but I'm glad I still have my kitten. We found Blacky in the feld tangled in bob wire 8 years ago and my brother's firend took him home but

Blacky didn't like him and his mom wouldn't let him keep Blacky, so we feed him and he wouldn't leav after that, his first meal with us was popcorn, the popcorn bag fell over and Blacky ran up and stared to eat the popcorn and when he got all the popcorn off the floor he stak his hade in the popcorn bag and he stared to eat the popcorn out of the bag and he finshed up the bag of popcorn, and when we tried to get the popcorn he would drag his [head] out of the bag and would mowe.

A recount such as this usually begins with an orientation to let the reader know something about the character and setting. In this case, it's an orientation to the composer's emotional response as well as the motivation for the recount. This is a story that needs telling, somehow, in order to complete it. The narrative itself comes next, beginning with "We found Blacky in the feld . . ." As they tumble out, these events contextualize the composer's emotional response, so that the reader can now place that against the images and the drama of the narrative. Recounts often end with a personal comment meant to bring some significance to the events that have been narrated (Derewianka, 1990). In this recount, it's the events themselves that make this comment, creating the picture of a hungry stray and telling us something about the emotional life of the narrator. The narrative and its images evidence the very depth of the composer's emotions.

Biographies, like other larger nonfiction narratives, are also written to explain or reveal something about the person or about the events being recounted (Ellis, 2000). What are we to learn about this particular life and why it was lived in this particular way? We read biography usually because the difficulties or the successes or the puzzles of a particular life intrigue us, instruct us, or resonate with us somehow. Perhaps children write biography for the same reasons, beginning with questions about their own lives, questions that others have similarly asked and tried to answer in their own ways. These are the questions we can ask children, certainly as they compose autobiography, but also as they assemble and focus biographies of others so that the uniqueness of a life emerges. That which fascinates or troubles—a way of thinking, living, expressing oneself—all of these have meaning beyond the surface level. The story of a life is told for a reason. Events are included because they reflect this reason, even if the reason itself is not yet articulated. Nonfiction narrative sometimes helps the child to articulate it.

Research Reports

Research reports that record and communicate experimental or laboratory studies often use a four-part format (Martin, 1993). This format also works for many other kinds of research projects that involve gathering information about a topic, such as observational studies, surveys, interviews, or reading the literature about a subject. These are the four parts:

- **Aim:** What is the object of the investigation? What is the question that the researcher wants to answer?
- **Method:** What procedure was used? What kind of apparatus was used? Who were the participants?
- **Results:** What happened? What were the data that you discovered? (Tables may be used to organize these results.)
- **Conclusion:** What are the general conclusions or laws that the results show? What is the significance of the results?

A child composer who experiments with dissolving substances, for example, could report on the investigation using this format. The report would open with a general statement that orients the reader to the aim, topic, or question that motivated the investigation (Derewianka, 1990). In this case, the composer was trying to find out which of a set of substances dissolve in water.

To do this, each child investigator in a kindergarten might use an apparatus consisting of a chem-plate, an eyedropper, four substances (sugar, salt, baking soda, and sand), and a cup of water. Next, the composer would describe the procedure: drip water onto each substance in the chem-plate and stir it a bit. This information goes into the method section of the report.

The findings or results follow the method, organized in paragraphs or sections according to topic—in this case, the results would separate the two types of reactions that the child observed. Both the method and the results are narrative in the sense that they tell what happened in the study, but not as an activity description does. The method describes a general procedure used for this experiment, not simply the actions performed by one individual. In much the same way, the results section lays out the patterns that the researcher found as the procedure was carried out. For example, the results of the dissolving experiment might show that sugar, salt, and baking soda dissolve but sand doesn't.

Young children may convey the results they observe through oral language alone, and not on the page at all. They may also devise emergent forms of tables, charts, or diagrams to summarize what they've seen, as in Scene 10, below. An essential question is whether or not the graphic organizers convey an accurate understanding or have helped the child to understand the information at an intermediate point. An oral reading of the data table with the child helps to assess the correspondence between the graphics on the page and the child's understanding. Sometimes both are inaccurate, but still logical within the child's frame of reasoning. Alternatively, the graphics may reflect an understanding that the child isn't yet able to articulate orally or through written text (Shepardson and Britsch, 2000).

The conclusion of the report brings together the significance of the results, indicating what the composer makes of these findings. The conclusion of this dissolving experiment might indicate, for example, that white substances dissolve and nonwhite substances don't. In this case, the conclusion isn't wrong; it reflects an accurate generalization based on the substances that the child was given: salt, sugar, baking soda, and sand. A sample including salt, sugar, sand, and soil would be less likely to lead to the inaccurate conclusion. This second set of substances could also be used to follow up the first experiment, adding complications that might dislodge the first conclusion. This setup is important because the conclusion of a report addresses the "so what" factor—the conclusion ties the report together, taking the composer beyond a simple listing of results to a more general statement about what they mean. Depending on the results, the composer may or may not be able to include a *why* explanation for them. An older child might, for example, add that the particles become smaller as substances dissolve.

Sometimes conclusions also suggest an application or use for the findings. Because this is really a separate issue, an additional section of the report may detail the study's implications for subsequent action in the world. Children frequently share the implications they discover after the investigation has piqued their awareness. They may have noticed, for example, that Mom dissolved sugar in her coffee this morning. They may also participate in teacher-provided experiences that reflect or contradict the conclusions of a report. This will lead to the kind of rereading and revising that scientists actually do.

Scene 10: Reporting Results with a Data Table.

In his kindergarten room, Jeffrey conducted an experiment to determine which of four substances in his chem-plate would dissolve in water: sugar, salt, sand, or soil. He used his science journal to record his findings, organizing these into an emergent form of a qualitative data table (Figure 3.7). It lacks only the headings that would characterize a true data table (Britsch, 2001b, p. 104).

Although he found the results for sugar, salt, and sand uninteresting, Jeffrey was intrigued by the reaction of his soil sample, which he wrote differently: DIRT was actually depicted as dirty! Because some small pebbles in his soil sample didn't dissolve, he

Figure 3.7 An emergent data table.

invented his own term to reflect a middle ground between dissolving and not-dissolving (Shepardson and Britsch, 2001, p, 54):

> The dirt is fracturing. Some parts of it are on top and some are on the bottom. It's different from dissolving.

Jeffrey's journal entry and talk show that he understood the phenomenon. He elaborated and described these results through his talk. He used two non-narrative genres to do this: he described his results and he classified them in an organized way using his data table. In this way, he presented what might be included in the "Results" section of a report. The next page of his journal might include a conclusion that he dictates or writes, such as, "Some substances dissolve and others don't." To add another section, his teacher might talk with him about the "Procedure," using that term. In this way, teachers can offer additional tools that researchers use to organize what they understand about an investigation. This provides a kind of cognitive modeling for the child that opens up new ways of thinking about science experiences—ways that are more elaborated than activity descriptions.

Children may also represent science activity by diagramming or listing the results of an observation or experiment. In the diagram shown in Figure 3.8, the composer indicated the materials, even including the term "soil," but concluded with "I like salt!," not with observed results.

The child's conclusion suggests that his procedure also included tasting some of the dissolved substances. In this case, the conclusion made personal sense, but not the general kind of sense that goes with the aim of the experiment. One issue that requires clarification, then, is whether or not the child understood the science concept. Next, clarifying the aim of the experiment with the child by asking, "What were we trying to find out?" might lead to a conclusion that keeps with the aim. This would begin to broaden the child's context from the here-and-now of his own activity to the more generalized there-and-then of the scientific experience (Genishi and Dyson, 1984).

In the following example (see Figure 3.9), an older composer verbally described her personal activity ("I saw some gold color in my dirt") and concluded with a subjective reaction ("It was really neat").

Here again, asking the composer to state the aim of the investigation might guide the child toward a conclusion that makes

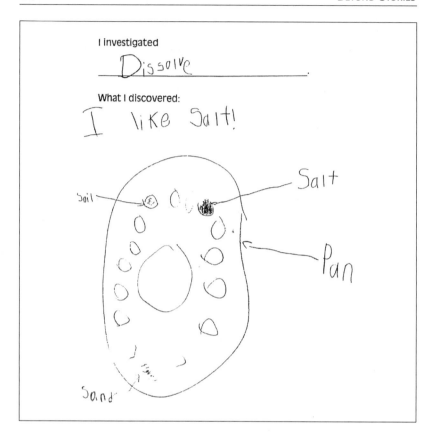

Figure 3.8 A kindergartener's diagram.

sense of something that interests her—the gold color she observed. This then suggests further, more objective, questions: why might soil be colored gold? What might have caused this? Further research could revisit this report as a middle ground to work from in preparing a next version. Scientists do this.

A conclusion stating the generalized meaning of the observations or activity in which the child has engaged is often missing from research reports, especially in science. Also, the method, or procedure, is often more implicit than explicit because the children have already enacted it through their own experience—it may not make sense to restate the obvious. Articulating the general aim of the experiment also casts the method as a generalized procedure, not just a personal action. This is not to diminish the

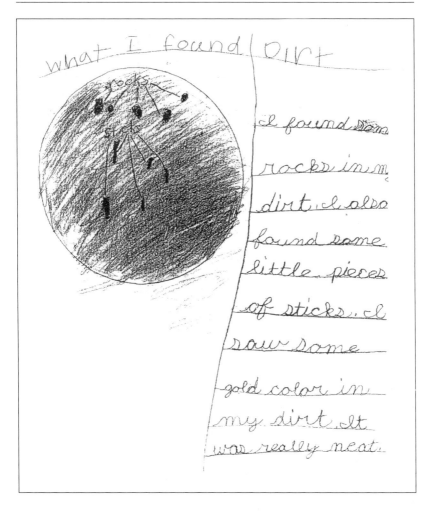

Figure 3.9 An older child's research report.

context that the child brings to an investigation, but to introduce an additional one. Different subject areas or areas of inquiry (e.g., science, history) organize reality according to different criteria (Martin, 1993). Knowing what to pay attention to gives children access to these perspectives. The new context gradually becomes more familiar as an internalized context, closing the distance between composer and subject.

Scene 11: Narrative Reporting.

When Deanna used her chem-plate to dissolve the four substances, she created an oral-drawn-written narrative to describe her results (Shepardson and Britsch, 2001, p. 54; see figure 3.10). She related her findings to a context inhabited by an animal character—a duck—that you'd find outdoors where sand and soil more naturally occur.

An oral narrative accompanied her graphic product (Britsch, 2001b, p. 102):

> She doesn't like that dirt mixing up with the sand between her toes because it's too messy and it's dissolving.

Figure 3.10 A narrative research report.

This is really quite a sophisticated linking of an outer context with another abstract context (the duck) that isn't visible at this moment. This is her sense-making process. Although this imaginary setting contextualized Deanna's understanding of dissolving, it might be based on inaccurate scientific information. Further explorations will clarify whether she views dirt and sand, or both, as dissolving substances—whether she understands the concept wholly.

Martin (1993) argues that imaginative writing distracts students from building scientific understandings. Imaginative writing does not explore the way that science interprets the world because it does not classify, measure, explain, or decompose. But it did for Deanna. She designed a genre to respond to a new situation by drawing on the resources she had. Isn't this learning?

Endnote

Real composing goes beyond distinct forms or structures. Teaching composing goes beyond handing children a template and asking them to fill it in. We observe the forms children devise to fit their own thinking and to capture what they've identified as the elements important to a situation. Teachers are looking to see what the children are working on, not to constrain them with their own conceptions of what that is or should be. The collection of composing choices shown here is meant to suggest ideas—things to watch for in order to appreciate the composer's purpose and effort. Teachers can suggest new options that will address the composers' needs, but we have to know where they've been in order to see where they're going. What questions or comments will hook into the existing set of cognitions and capacities that a composer brings to a task? What is the composer is trying to do with drawing, talk, and writing? What is the context from which that emerged?

The novelist Maxine Hong Kingston has said, "I feel that the writing process doesn't just begin when you are putting words on paper. It begins in the living you do before" (Seshachari, 1998, p. 198). The classroom adds another layer of context to this "living before." This is the focus of the next chapter.

Chapter 4

"What Happens to the BEE?"

Children Composing Nonfiction in Classrooms

The Range of Response

Teaching that allows only one kind of response really isn't fair. The child has no stake in it. When the scene surrounding the page changes, when a letter becomes a cry of sadness about a missing pet, that's when writing becomes necessary and dynamic—a personal possession. The nonfiction composing of very young children often helps them participate in an experience as it's happening—we've seen tickets, warnings, and prescriptions do this. Children who link experience, imagination, and investigation to their composing create different ways of participating in the event itself. The next sections illustrate classroom projects in which teachers elicited and responded to the contexts that the children brought, and then created scenes that stretched these contexts to broaden the children's nonfiction composing capabilities. These scenes portray the expansion of children's composing choices over time in the context of an investigation that is suggested by the children's interests and guided by the teachers. The first series of scenes focuses on Jack, a six-year-old with a budding knowledge of insects—bees, in particular. These scenes took place over a number of days. It took time each day for Jack to work carefully through the kind of detailed work he was doing. His progression illustrates a way of working with an individual child over time to develop nonfiction composing based on, but broadening, the composer's interests.

Jack

Jack was six years and four months old. He loved bugs, and he knew a lot about them, too. He especially knew a lot about bees and he communicated this through very detailed drawing, accompanied by talk. To build this knowledge, his teacher created a very open-ended situation where she provided lots of different kinds of paper along with pencils, markers, and colored pencils. In a nondirective, open-ended way, and without stipulating a medium, she asked Jack to "create two texts—something that you know a lot about."

Scene 1

In response, Jack created a pencil drawing that caught a bee in midflight from its hive to a flower. Each element of his drawing was very detailed: the bee with its three body parts, wings, and legs, the honeycombed hive, and even the flight path of the bee (two wispy lines through the air). Jack then composed an oral text that began with a bit of narrative (Figure 4.1):

> What is happening here is that the bee is coming from its hive to the flower to get pollen and nectar. There's the difference between pollen and nectar. Pollen is this powdery stuff. Nectar is the liquidy stuff that is inside flowers. Like I picked a dandelion and when I squeezed the stem, some nectar came out. But I didn't keep it . . . 'cause I don't know how to make honey. The bees do.

The first sentence narrates the bee's activity in Jack's drawing: "What is happening here is that the bee is coming from its hive to the flower to get pollen and nectar." Although this language also describes the specific bee Jack has drawn, he probably understands that it also describes bee behavior in general, and not simply the individual activity of a single character-like bee. He next adds a pair of descriptions that contrast the physical attributes of pollen and nectar. He closes with a description of his own past activity, but the dandelion in it actually works as an example to further illustrate the difference between pollen and nectar.

In this drawn-spoken composition, Jack characterizes bees as a group of creatures with their own set of attributes and habits. His teacher had heard him use the word "bugs" as a generic term for all insects. Has he understood that the bees are one of many types of insects? If so, can he broaden his knowledge of these various types? His interest and his affinity for detail might lend themselves to a non-narrative genre: a classification based on concrete details that Jack can observe.

Scene 2

Jack's teacher next brought in large photographs of some arthropods: the insects, arachnids, myriapods, and crustaceans that have jointed limbs. She and Jack also looked at some diagrams

Figure 4.1 Jack's first bee composition.

of arthropods in factual books. Then Jack went back to the photographs. He proceeded to move them into groups according to the number of wings each creature had. His teacher also brought along several different kinds of paper: blank paper, index cards, a booklet of blank paper, and some graph paper covered with one-inch squares. Jack first chose the index cards and wrote headings on them for each of his categories: "4 wengs," "2 wengs," and "No wings." He placed each heading above the appropriate set of pictures. Next, he made the graph paper into a chart, incorporating the headings from his index cards. Based on the photographs he'd looked at, he drew each creature in a different cell of

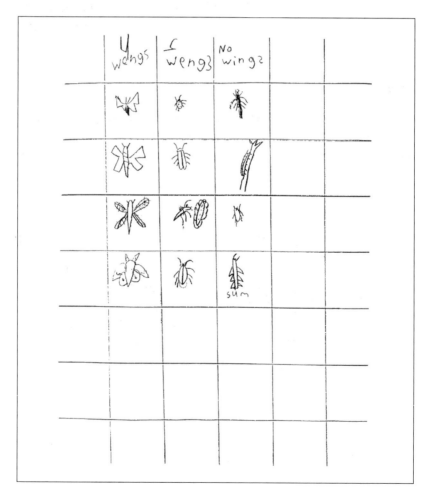

Figure 4.2 Jack's insect classification.

the appropriate column on his chart. The chart is shown in figure 4.2.

When Jack "read" his chart back, he orally labeled each drawing; for example, he pointed to the drawings under "4 wengs" and said, "This is the monarch, the swallowtail, dragonfly, and moth." These labels all focused on insects. Although he didn't comment on it, he also drew the correct number of legs for most of his examples. Jack had developed a labeled classification, detailed through his drawings.

Scene 3

Next, as a kind of post-activity, Jack's teacher asked him to show something he had learned about insects. This time, she specified the focus for his composing. Using a sheet of paper and a blue marker, Jack now conveyed what he knew using written language alone:

All bugs have antennas. Not all bugs have wings. All bugs have disguise. Some bugs like to eat flowers.

Jack's concept list here (Figure 4.3) reflects the inductive logic he's used, going from the parts to the whole to create generalizations about insects. In terms of science content, we'd still want to

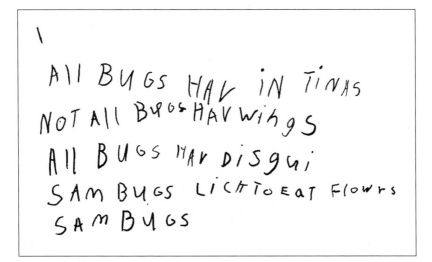

Figure 4.3 Jack's concept list.

make sure that he doesn't think all insects are technically "bugs". We could also explore some of the other terms he's used; "disguise" is particularly intriguing and could lead to further drawn and written description.

In Scene 2, Jack's labels all focused on insects, which are arthropods. Perhaps, we could now broaden this focus and use an emergent kind of taxonomy to connect insects with other groups within the larger grouping of arthropods. This might reflect, for example, the similarities and differences between insects and myriapods such as centipedes and millipedes. Jack's teacher might introduce the tree diagram as an organizer, placing the photographs differently (i.e., not in columns this time) to elaborate his classification. Jack might introduce his index-card labels into this process as well. The tree diagram is another way in which scientists reflect their view of the world (Martin, 1993), and it might expand Jack's way of seeing details and relating them to something larger.

This teacher built on the child's initial response by critically selecting materials based on her awareness of his knowledge and on her own awareness of the genres appropriate to science (Tyler, 1949). Had she not begun with a very open-ended diagnostic composing situation, she might not have offered the specific materials she did. They directed Jack's initial interest and allowed him to optimally use his knowledge, which led to his classification. Had she stopped at that point, she might not have observed his ability to compose in written sentences. Changes in purpose motivate changes in genre as well as changes in the forms of emergent writing that children use for different kinds of texts (Zecker, 1999). By providing a variety of contexts for composing, teachers can observe and expand the range of children's composing abilities.

The following series of scenes move to a third grade classroom where the students developed a fascination with bees that was based on fiction but pursued it through nonfiction.

A Nonfiction Investigation in Third Grade

This next set of scenes comes from a third-grade classroom where a whole-class project centered on bees. These children approached the topic after reading a fictional narrative. The project promoted student-initiated questioning, not a transmission of facts to the children. The children found real answers to their questions, and these were not derived from a preset list of answers that the teacher had already determined would be "discovered." The children's learning thus drove the unit, but the change evolved over time. Here are the scenes that took place.

Scene 1

To begin, the students read the first chapter of *A Taste of Blackberries* (Smith, 1973), a novel that deals with death by accident. Instead of focusing the initial discussion about the book on recall questions about the characters or the setting, this teacher aimed to create student-centered interest by focusing on questions that *they* had. She asked for their questions, and as she listed these on the board, she discovered that the children didn't seem to be interested in death at all, contrary to her predictions. She then talked with the children about the different kinds of questions they had compiled. Many were actually recall questions that could have been answered by referring to the chapter (e.g., when the story took place). Others were meant to "clarify confusion" (e.g., what was meant by a particular phrase) (Harvey, 1998, p. 29). Others, however, were inference questions with answers that had to be surmised from the information contained in the novel (Harvey, 1998). None required any research beyond the novel. These questions required experience with a different kind of thought process. Sometimes composers need to change the kinds of tasks they "give themselves" (Flower, 1990, p. 226). In other words, do composers see themselves as "summarizers" or as "explicators" (Flower, 1990, p. 226)? As reproducers or as questioners?

Scene 2

After the class read the second chapter of the novel, the teacher talked with the children about some research questions that might be based on topics or ideas mentioned in the chapter. She gave some examples of questions that required research beyond the text to illustrate the differences between the types of questions that were appropriate to this new purpose (Harvey, 1998). The students then worked in pairs to devise two of their own research questions.

In Chapter 2 of the novel, the children get caught in a thunderstorm. This theme was present in many of the questions. Blackberries (not specifically mentioned in the chapter) were the second most popular theme:

+ How hot is lightning?
+ What is lightning made of?
+ What can you make with blackberries?
+ Where do blackberries grow?

Although these questions do require research and reading beyond the novel, many can be answered briefly with single-word responses or lists of items (e.g., foods to prepare using blackberries). The questions about blackberries reflect one of the settings, but not the theme, of the novel. Those about lightning reflect one of the minor events in the story and perhaps a fascination or fear of some of the children. The most complex question was a heuristic one: "What makes thunderstorms?" This one would require a *why* explanation.

The next day, the class brainstormed questions that could be drawn from Chapter 3 of the novel, in which one of the characters experiences an allergic reaction to a bee sting and is taken to the hospital. This scene motivated most of the children's new questions, but with a twist. The children were less interested in what happened to the human character than in what happens to a bee after it stings someone. The children also posed other questions:

+ What makes a person allergic to bee stings?
+ If someone is allergic to one type of bee, are they allergic to all bees?
+ What makes a bee sting someone?

These were more complex questions, requiring *why* explanations to answer them. The children began their research with the encyclopedia, but many questions remained unanswered because the encyclopedia simply did not contain that kind of information. The children concluded that they needed to look beyond the encyclopedia to books with titles about bees and allergies. Keeping their list of questions at hand, the children read. If the book or article did not answer their questions, they would brainstorm ideas with their teacher about how to find the answers elsewhere. This created an environment that encouraged the children to develop new roles for themselves as questioners and researchers.

Scene 3

Through the development of their own questions, the children were now beginning to discover which kinds required a synthesis of information from several sources and which simply called for lists of facts that could be summarized from a single source. They worked in small groups to refine their questions and then came together to classify their questions into categories by theme, eliminating those that didn't require any further research. They found that the two most popular themes in the class were bee stings and allergic reactions. These two nonfiction topics were drawn from the novel's central conflict: the reaction of one of the characters to the death of another character as the result of a bee sting. These two topics would help the children in this classroom to discover *why*. They wanted science information that would explain one kind of unusual, apparently random occurrence in the world. This was not a teacher assigned focus. The children questioned the *cause* of the death in the novel, not the emotional or coping aspects of such a situation. They sought answers in scientific information. They combed the Internet, checked out books from the public and school libraries, and interviewed the school nurse.

Scene 4

After specifying their questions and doing a great deal of reading, the children had findings in hand. They next had to decide how best to represent the information they'd accumulated. These are the kinds of genre choices writers make based on their intentions (Wiley, 2000). The general intention of these composers was to present information. To serve this expository purpose, however, these composers recruited various narrative and non-narrative devices. Based on suggestions, not rules, from their teacher, the children made five primary composing choices.

One choice was a list, as shown in Figure 4.4. As a composing choice, this is much more than a list of words. Grammatically it is a sentence list, but each item conveys a concept, a more fully expressed idea. Overall, these are sequentially ordered, beginning with the cause of bee stings and continuing with a possible consequence to allergic victims. Items 3 and 4 focus on the bee's characteristics, but item 4 links these back to the process of a bee sting. The list ends with information about medication for persons allergic to bee stings. In other words, although it takes the form of a concept list, this piece accomplishes the function (and contains many of the features) of a *how* explanation. It also has a narrative quality about it, although the composer chose a non-narrative genre for this expository purpose. This composer knows how to use language for much more than a narrative function.

Other children represented what they'd learned through an interview with the bee, as shown in Figure 4.5.

Figure 4.4 A sentence-list of ordered concepts about bees.

Although it's in the form of a script, this composing choice has an expository purpose. It also focuses on some different topics than the list in Figure 4.4. The interview composer carries out several language functions using a question-and-answer format. Although three of the interviewer's five questions are yes/no questions, the bee answers them more fully. The first questions a condition: "If you are allergic to bees, are you allergic to all bees?" The response replaces the second clause of the question with a confirming statement, a generalization about these types of allergies: "You are allergic to all bees, wasps, and yellow jackets." The second yes/no question ("Is there a medicine to help you if you

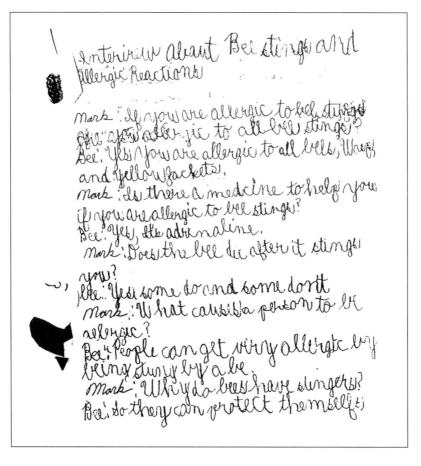

Figure 4.5 A bee interview.

are allergic to bee stings?") is answered with a label. The bee answers the third with a phrase that qualifies its "yes" response ("Some do and some don't"). The fourth question is really a why question: "What causes a person to be allergic?" The bee answers: "People can get very allergic by being stung by a bee." This is a partial *why* explanation. An allergen causes an allergic reaction, but why are some people allergic to bee stings and others not? An audience might expect the answer to that question instead. The next question ("Why do bees have stingers?") also requires a *why* explanation, which the bee provides. This last question seems to switch topics, but it might be linked to the previous answer in the composer's mind. This wouldn't necessarily be clear to an audience, however.

This interview format points up some issues of audience expectation and response to exposition. An oral dramatization in the classroom might engage the precise use of question types through the questions asked by an informed group of co-researchers. For example, the third yes/no question ("Does the bee die after it stings you?") can't be fully answered with a simple affirmative or negative. It might be amended to, "Do all bees die after they sting someone?" This is more likely to result in description and/or classification that expands the bee's already qualified answer. Finally, although the interview subject is the bee itself, the interviewer questions it about the human experience of a bee sting as well as the bee's experience in general. This might open up some possibilities for exploring point of view in writing.

Other composers took a further step toward synthesis by relating pieces of information in a web, as shown in Figure 4.6.

The focal theme of this web is "Bees and Being Allergic." The composer refines this by classifying his information into categories: (a) "stingers," (b) "medicine," (c) "What causes you to be allergic," (d) "If you are allergic to bees are you allergic to all bees," and (e) "Does the bee die after it stings you?" The bubbles connected to these topics then provide relevant facts. This non-narrative classification synthesizes a corpus of information, and reflects something about the composer's thinking process. Although a web is not typically a conventional form for representing scientific data (Shepardson and Britsch, 2001), this one organizes information in a way that the child can understand. In fact, a non-narrative form such as a web or tree diagram often

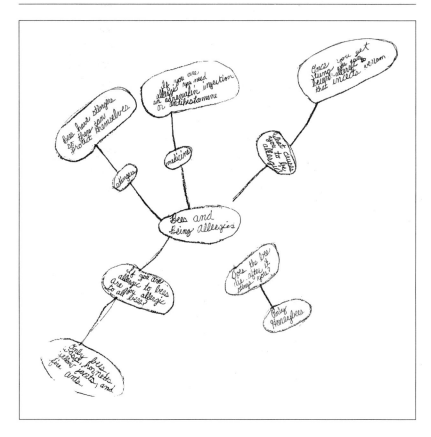

Figure 4.6 A classification in the form of a web.

helps composers to see the connections and gaps between ideas. Because these pieces of information are derived from each other, however, this composer might also have constructed a tree diagram with a main heading at the top and branches to subcategories (Moline, 1995). This kind of choice helps composers turn new findings into familiar information by grappling with ideas and organizing them to reflect the aim of the investigation. A next step might be to research the kinds of structures that would allow the composer to elaborate these single-fact statements in a research report relating the various pieces of information (Martin, 1993).

Other composers in this classroom chose a form that directly conveys information from one individual to another. These children composed letters, as shown in Figure 4.7.

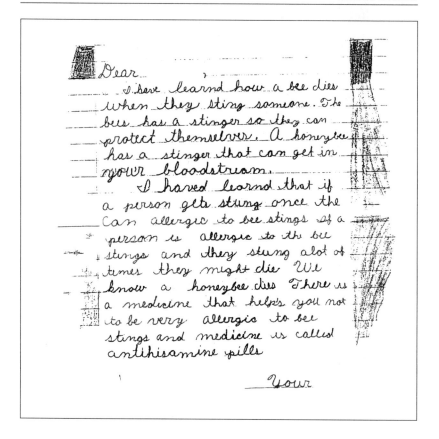

Dear   ,
          I have learnd how a bee dies
    when they sting someone. The
    bee has a stinger so they can
    protect themselves. A honeybee
    has a stinger that can get in
    your bloodstream.
          I haved learnd that if
    a person gets stung once the
    Can allergic to bee stings of a
    person is allergic to the bee
    stings and they stung alot of
    times they might die We
    know a honeybee dies There is
    a medicine that helps you not
    to be very allergic to bee
    stings and medicine is called
    antihisamine pills

                              Your

Figure 4.7 An informational letter.

The first paragraph of this letter contains several ideas about bees, clustered around the topic of "stingers" and "stinging." This gives the paragraph an almost listlike quality. There are several compelling facts in the first paragraph, however, that suggest elaboration. The first sentence indicates that the composer has learned "how a bee dies when they sting someone." This might be elaborated with a *how* explanation (i.e., a bee dies when the stinger comes out of its body). This would set up a topic sentence for the paragraph, supported with a logically related explanation. The composer might choose to continue the same pattern with the remaining ideas in the paragraph. In contrast, the second paragraph orders four central ideas sequentially, beginning with (1) how people acquire an allergy to bee stings, and moving to (2) the possible consequence of death if people with allergies are stung multiple times. The paragraph pursues the topic of death by suggesting that (3) although the bee dies, (4) antihistamines can help humans. In this case, the composer has combined several pieces of information to describe a process in depth. It's a kind of *how* explanation that reads almost like a narrative with a remedy, or resolution, at the end. This provides a structure that could also work to smooth out the conceptual order of the ideas in the first paragraph. The composer will need to distinguish the forms that most effectively suit the different purposes in these paragraphs.

Other children composed research reports to represent their findings:

What Bees And Allergies Really Are.

- You can be allergic to many things and one of the most deadly things to be allergic to is the bee.

There are three ways to become allergic to bees. One way to become allergic to bees is if you get stong, once you can't become allergic. Anther way to become allergic is if you are old and get stong you can become allergic easyer than younger people. The last way to become allergic is if your parents are allergic you can be allergic too.

There are many different bees that you can be allergic to. If you are allergic to bees you are allergic to all types of bee, wasps, and yellow jakets and hornits.

If you are allergic to bees, don't be afraid there is medicine that you can take it is an adrenaline injection or antihistamini pills if you are allergic you should wear a Medic Alert bracelet.

If you ever get stong by a bee you should do the following, go to a docter and see if you are allergic. If you are allergic you should get adreneline injection or antihistamine pills, and you should wear a Medic Alet Bracelet and stay away from all bees, wasps, yellow jakets and hornets.

Figure 4.8 A classification in the form of a research report.

The composition shown in Figure 4.8 opens with a general statement, focusing the piece on allergies to the bee (see "Research Reports" in Chapter 3). The report then lists three ways of becoming allergic to bees: "one way," "another way," "the last way." Then it moves to a new issue: types of bees, and a piece of related information about allergies to all types of bees. The next paragraph takes up remedies for the allergic person. The final paragraph lists practical steps to take in case of a bee sting. This composer has logically classified a series of topics under a general rubric. This reflects the strength of the composer's classification.

Even though they take different forms, all of the composing choices shown above respond to the children's need to know *why* the character in *A Taste of Blackberries* died. They all address this central function or purpose, the heart of a self-focused inquiry. This composing was not first a question of form, but one of purpose and intention. These composers selected or modified non-narrative forms for an expository purpose in imaginative, engaging, and effective ways. The teacher's emphasis was on engaging student choice, not on getting through a set of teacher-planned activities. The children's various composing choices reflected this respect for individual perspective.

In this project, the teacher's primary aim was not to teach a particular canon, but to develop the children's ability to express an interest and design an investigation to follow it up. To accomplish it, she focused less on her own actions in the classroom and more on the children's inquiry process. This, in turn, made the children's composing into a very active and direct engagement with the subject matter, and generated a range of composing choices. Nonfiction and non-narrative genres became ways of perpetuating activity—ways that were organic to that activity for its participants. The notion of "audience" also became much less closely identified with "teacher." It expanded to include peers, not just as friends, but as other researchers, readers, and questioners.

The kinds of questions that structure children's investigations can also focus response and composing choice. The next section of this chapter will present several different types of question and some of the ways in which these suggest a range of composing choices.

Questioning for Composing

The way in which a question for investigation is posed can suggest a more or less complex kind of response. When posed one way, a question may generate a one-word response. When posed another way, the question offers more possibilities for elaboration using multiple genres. The response itself also becomes more or less complex depending upon (a) the nature of the interaction between the composer and the teacher or peers, and (b) the breadth of the composer's awareness of different composing choices. This requires an ability to approach problems and design questions that lead to in-depth investigation and further thinking. We hope that children are constantly developing their ability to question as their composing progresses. They can then become evaluators of their own questions, though they may often be helped by the teacher and by peers. Well-designed questions suggest different ways of thinking about and exploring a problem, and thus generate different responses.

Table 4.1 suggests phrasings for several question types that may lend themselves more or less usefully to complex kinds of response, conveyed through a composing choice or choices. A child's response may require the use of more than one composing choice; alternatively, the composer may go beyond the choices shown here. The table is not meant to convey a normative progression or a sequence for instruction; instead, it is intended as a guide that teachers can use to make decisions about questioning for composing. Each of the question types is described below.

Yes/No Questions

It's probably not a good question if answer is simply "yes" or "no." A more useful question allows the composer to explain or describe; for example, "Are ladybugs insects?" actually requires an explanation that relies on classification of a ladybug as an insect. On the other hand, "Do insects have six legs?" doesn't require the composer to classify anything; it merely requires knowing whether insects have six legs or not.

Table 4.1. Some Question Types and Possible Composing Choices

QUESTION TYPE	EXAMPLE QUESTION	COMPOSING CHOICES THE QUESTION SUGGESTS
Yes/no questions	**More useful:** "Are ladybugs insects?" ++++++++ **Less useful:** "Do insects have six legs?"	Description *Why*-explanation Classification ++++++++ Affirmative or negative response
Single-word-answer questions	**More useful:** "What other mammal is a guinea pig like?" ++++++++ **Less useful:** "What type of mammal is a guinea pig?"	Classification Description *Why*-explanation ++++++++ Single word Classification
Listing questions	**More useful:** "How do raccoon tracks differ from dog tracks?" ++++++++ **Less useful:** "How many types of animal tracks indicate a hoofed animal?"	Classification *Why*-explanation Description ++++++++ Numerical response List
Observation questions	**More useful:** "How will the playground change in the next two weeks this fall?" ++++++++ **Less useful:** "How long does it take leaves to change color?"	*How*-explanation *Why*-explanation Narrative Description ++++++++ Numeral or phrase
Heuristic questions	**More useful:** "How do different microscope lenses help you see things differently?" ++++++++ **Less useful:** "How does a microscope work?"	*Why*-explanation *How*-explanation Classification Activity description Object description ++++++++ Single phrase. *How*-explanation
Research questions	**More useful:** "What happens to a bee after it stings you?" ++++++++ **Less useful:** "How many kinds of bees are there?"	Research report Nonfiction narrative *Why*-explanation ++++++++ List

Single-Word-Answer Questions

Although we may not realize it, many of the questions we typically ask children—even some *"how"* and *"why"* questions—can be answered with what is essentially a single-word response. A question such as "How do snakes move?" can be reduced to "They slither." Usually, however, it's *"what"* questions that lead to single-word responses. For example, "What type of mammal is a guinea pig?" may elicit simply "A rodent." If pursued further, a classification of mammals could result. These two steps alone may be useful for some students, but to expand the answers further, the question could be amended to "What other mammal is a guinea pig like?" This inquiry could begin in any number of ways and would require observation leading to description, and literature research leading to classification or *why* explanation.

Listing Questions

Questions that are likely to produce lists of items are not always productive for young children. Developmentally, young children have "relatively poor recall of list-like information that is not embedded in meaningful contexts" (Bredekamp and Copple, 1997, p. 113). But lists can be more or less elaborate. If they are not limited to labels or phrases but instead detail qualities about objects, creatures, or environments, composers can relate individual qualities to a whole entity or context. This helps in structuring ideas (Humphryes, 2000, p. 18). A question such as "How many types of animal tracks indicate a hoofed animal?" could lead to a numerical answer or to a list of animal names. A more specific question would be "How do raccoon tracks differ from dog tracks?" This could elicit detailed description or classification that would link these two animals to a larger group.

Observation Questions

Questions can refine children's observation skills. By focusing on a particular topic or environment, observation questions can generate object descriptions through language or labeled diagrams, *how* explanations, activity descriptions, or nonfiction narratives. An observation question such as "How long does it take leaves to change color?" requires a long observation period that can be recorded in a log, but essentially it requires only a numerical conclusion. A question that holds more potential for response expansion could be "How will the playground change in the next two weeks this fall?" This would require the observation of a bounded, familiar environment for specific changes and contrasts during a specified period of time (Tallmadge, 2000). This is focused, concrete, and manageable and suggests a variety of composing choices: narrative, description, *how* explanation, *why* explanation, or a combination of these.

Heuristic Questions

Heuristic questions engage children's thinking about how things work. They can, therefore, motivate *how* and *why* explanations. The usefulness of the question, however, also depends upon how much the children are truly able to understand about the phenomenon. Magnetic attraction can be observed and classifications derived by kindergartners, but the role of iron in the process can't be accommodated in terms of their physical and concrete way of learning (see Chapter 3). Heuristic questions can also be posed very broadly: "How does a microscope work?" This suggests a *how* explanation or possibly a nonfiction narrative, but if scientific thinking is the aim, the composer's response can be focused more precisely. The question then becomes "How do microscope lenses help you to see things differently?" This suggests systematic observation that may lead to description or classification, *how* explanation or *why* explanation.

Research Questions

Research questions tend to be most useful if the researchers themselves recognize the problem or question and provide the cognitive focus. In this case, "*how*" and "*why*" questions usually call for more explanation and/or description, but not all "*how*" and "*why*" questions are good ones. For example, "Why do leaves change color?" may be too broad and too abstract for younger children, as well as for some older children. "How do leaves change color?" may suggest a *how* explanation, but if the aim is a *why* explanation, the composer has to be able to reason it out instead of simply rephrasing an explanation from another source. Although *how* questions, which focus on processes and procedures, may seem more accessible, some concepts may be too abstract. For example, "How are elephants related to mastodons?" requires a great deal of abstract reasoning based only on print sources, not on direct observation or physical learning. On the opposite end of the spectrum, "How many kinds of bees are there?" merely requires counting a list of names or pictures.

As we've seen in this chapter, the most useful research questions are those that are developed by the children. Throughout this process, teachers constantly assess and restructure the goals and subgoals of the children's activity (Rogoff, 1990, p. 94). This helps children to see how different composing choices fit their activity, their own discovery processes, and their own knowledge. In terms of cognitive development, Barbara Rogoff has pointed out that this helps children to maintain their involvement:

> Involvement in the overall process and purpose of the activity, in a manageable and supported form, gives children a chance to see how the steps fit together and to participate in aspects of the activity that reflect the overall goals, gaining both skill and a vision of how and why the activity works (Rogoff, 1990, pp. 94–95).

Within the context of an investigation, the children's composing choices mirror their ways of participating in the experience. Each participant brings to the event a different set of assumptions, interests, and thinking processes. In choosing a genre, composers are doing more than simply reproducing convention; they are demonstrating their involvement, their investment, in the event. They are shaping their responses into forms that give others access to this response. Simply having information about conventional forms isn't enough because genre "responds to context" (Kress, 1999, p. 465) This chapter concludes with a set of questions meant to guide teachers in their creation of opportunities for nonfiction response in classrooms for young children.

Questions for Teachers

The first question for teachers is, how does literacy relate to the sense-making process for each child? How does the child *make* it make sense? Here are some other questions to ask when considering ways to extend a child's questioning, reasoning, investigating, and writing capacities.

- Does the question call for original thinking on the part of the composer?
- Will the response be more than a random or token list of items?
- Would the question generate *how* explanations?
- Can the issue really generate a *why* explanation for children at this developmental stage?
- Is the focus of the question too broad or too abstract?
- Can the question be answered through the child's own observation?
- Does the question require synthesis of information or simply a summary of information?
- Are the research findings concrete and specific enough for the child to make the connections needed for a synthesis?
- Is the context oversystematized so that all responses must be funneled into one particular composing choice, or are the tasks and investigations complex enough to invite a variety of composing choices?
- Which composing choices might the investigation or activity realistically motivate?
- How much does the composer understand about the situation?
- Which composing choice(s) more clearly communicate what the composer knows (e.g., a list, a classification, an explanation)?
- Which questions, beyond recall or comprehension questions, will guide the children in elaborating a response they've generated, offering a cognitive map and suggesting a composing choice?
- Can I talk the composer through the organization of a composing choice? For example, in organizing a report:
  - What's the most important thing you're telling the audience about?
  - How could we begin in a way that tells the audience what you're going to talk about here?

♦ How many different kinds of information are you giving?

♦ What else might your audience ask you about this fact or idea?

♦ Does that information come next in your composing?

Another question for the teacher to consider is "What is the composing process for each child?"

Some children may combine drawing or writing with talk. Asking about it after the fact misses all of the action that the composer is creating in the moment (Dyson, 1986). For other children, drawn or written composing may be a silent activity followed up with talk. As teachers observe children's composing behavior with different genres, they might even note different processes for the same composer.

Teachers' awareness of different composing options also enables them to assess a composer's current understanding and adjust their support. Composers, in turn, guide teachers in these supportive efforts (Rogoff, 1990). This approach to developing knowledge of genres is not best carried out by a pseudo-scaffolding with which the teacher "shapes" the piece and elicits a predictable outcome. Teachers can't *make* children produce a classification just because it's science. But if teachers value the capacity to choose a purpose and figure out how to achieve it, the composers in their classrooms need the power to choose a response. This requires a good deal of cognitive flexibility on the part of both teacher and learner. It requires both parties to develop a sense of audience and to see themselves as originators. As Linda Flower has pointed out, this transformation of knowledge cannot be imposed from without:

> Transformation appears to be a complex cognitive process that is heavily influenced by the plans and goals writers give themselves, which in turn are highly dependent on the support and incentives for such effort provided by the context (Flower, 1990, p. 225).

This doesn't happen quickly. We can shape the way, but this kind of growth means negotiation (Flower, 1990). Teachers can't impose the cognitive, emotional, or literate starting point for a child. Teachers can't dictate purpose to children. Teachers can structure scenes that help children to think in a variety of ways and enact a range of social, cognitive, and literate roles.

In the age of standards, the desire for uniform knowledge produced on schedule may seem to define learning, but this is antithetical to an educational aim of coping flexibly in new ways with new situations. This is, most essentially, what genre is all about. We take up reading as another type of response in the next chapter.

Chapter 5

The Role of Reading

In Nonfiction Composition

Reading as Response

A fearful idea now suddenly drove the blood in torrents upon my heart, and for a brief period I once more relapsed into insensibility. Upon recovering, I at once started to my feet, trembling convulsively in every fibre. I thrust my arms wildly above and around me in all directions. I felt nothing; yet dreaded to move a step, lest I should be impeded by the walls of a *tomb*. Perspiration burst from every pore, and stood in cold big beads upon my forehead. The agony of suspense grew at length intolerable, and I cautiously moved forward, with my arms extended, and my eyes straining from their sockets in the hope of catching some faint ray of light. I proceeded for many paces; but still all was blackness and vacancy. I breathed more freely. It seemed evident that mine was not, at least, the most hideous of fates (Poe, 1999, p. 344).

How did you react to this opening? What did you visualize? Or smell? Or sense? How did the author draw you into the drama of the situation he's created on the page?

Reading, like writing, is not a passive activity. We respond to what we read. In the case of narrative, we may respond by visualizing or by experiencing emotional changes because the text suggests images, memories, tensions, and even sensations to us. The elements that the writer details in a fictional narrative, for example, interact with our own emotions and memories to create another reality (Rosenblatt, 1988). Of course, readers also respond to nonfiction narratives. A reader might identify with the narrative of a life as it is characterized in a biography, for example. We also respond to the non-narrative texts we read, such as the following:

> It is useful to contrast heat energy to kinetic and gravitational energy, both of which are called *mechanical energy*. The energy of a swinging pendulum is an example of mechanical energy. The kinetic energy of any large object, all of whose parts are moving together in bulk, is called mechanical energy. In the case of the swinging pendulum, the pendulum bob contains many molecules moving together in bulk. This energy is to be distinguished from *heat* energy, the energy of the random motions of molecules. The gravitational energy of an object is also called *mechanical energy*, since such energy can be converted into the bulk motion of the object (after the release of a pendulum, for example). The slowing down of a pendulum illustrates mechanical energy turning into heat energy (Lightman, 2000, p. 82).

This particular text, a piece of non-narrative exposition, also evokes a response—one in which the reader formulates a mental classification that distinguishes heat energy from mechanical energy. The latter is then broken down into two types: kinetic energy and gravitational energy. It's a classification. The devices used in the text aid another of its functions: explanation. It illustrates the central concept, mechanical energy, with a concrete example. This might lead the reader to visualize a pendulum or the random motion of imaginary molecules. Because it's not a narrative, however, it doesn't convey a particular point of view about the topic.

In non-narrative texts, readers expect different elements than they do in narratives. Readers pick out the main points and the important points, and link them together (Flower, 1990, p. 246). They try to fit these points into an overall concept of what the piece is about. They don't do this by looking for characters. They don't look for setting. Although they connect ideas, steps, or processes, they don't look for a plot that is "deliberately arranged to reveal their dramatic, thematic, and emotional significance" (Burroway, 1996, p. 40).

Readers compose a mental picture, or structure, organizing the information in the text for themselves based on their expectations and their understanding. Reading is part of composing because it provides experience with and knowledge about non-narrative and narrative texts. "One must be an inventor to read well," says Harold Bloom (2000, p. 25). Just as we are inventors when we read fiction, we invent or construct connections when we read nonfiction and non-narrative texts. We link one point to another, and to what we already know, what we bring to the text. In this way, children's reading supports their composing. Teachers help children to be inventive readers who make these connections as they read. We help children to understand how different texts are structured. This gives children competence as efficient and inventive readers for different purposes.

One study of college-level writers presented students with an open-ended writing task that required them to be more "creative," drawing on the work of various novelists to critically evaluate the source texts (Kantz, 1987, as cited in Flower, 1990, p. 226). The factors that predicted good papers were not only the extent of the students' planning but also

> the students' purposeful use of reading strategies which let them select rhetorically relevant information and begin their constructive process as writers even as they read through the sources (Flower, 1990, p. 226).

Of course, children can't do this without well-constructed narrative and non-narrative texts to read and compare. This kind of critical literacy can happen early on; for example, children can read both narrative and non-narrative texts about the same topic, as did the children who investigated bees in Chapter 4. Then they can compare the organization of these texts as well as the kinds of information they contain. As the children read, or are read to, they make connections that the text suggests. Teachers can help by creating reading scenes to show children how to use texts in

An Exercise for Teacher and Student

Read one of your favorite pieces of narrative. What are some of the elements we look for in narrative? Ask yourself the same kinds of questions we typically ask children about stories (fictional narratives), for example:

+ Who is the protagonist? The antagonist?
+ How does the vocabulary convey feeling?
+ What is the conflict in the plot?
+ How do the characters resolve this conflict?
+ How would you feel if you found yourself in this situation?
+ How would *you* like the story to end?

Now apply these same questions to a piece of non-narrative writing, a technical explanation, for example. How many can we successfully answer? The questions listed above are, of course, not appropriate to the non-narrative writing that characterizes many fields of inquiry. They are not appropriate to science, for example, because they do not classify, measure, or explain or decompose findings (Martin, 1993).

Did you read the two pieces in the same way? Probably not.

+ Where did you look in order to identify the purpose(s) of the text?
+ What did you read next?
+ Which elements did you expect to find in the text?
+ How did you use the information you have about the genre?
+ Did you look for the headings and subheadings in a classification?
+ Did you check the order of the steps in a *how* explanation?
+ Did you first look at the conclusion of a research report and then compare this with the aim?

While we do ask some of the same questions of both narrative and non-narrative texts, they will be answered differently. By helping children to recognize these different answers, we help to develop genre knowledge. In addition, we take them beyond a word-by-word reading of every text they encounter.

different ways for different purposes. It's simply not efficient to read every single word of every single text.

Selecting Texts for Focused Reading

Teachers can explore this aspect of reading with children by providing examples of professional texts (for instance, a science journal article) and reading these in a focused way that reveals their distinctive characteristics. First, teachers need to examine individual texts in several ways. Table 5.1 lists some questions teachers can ask themselves about the content, text features, and illustrations in nonfiction and non-narrative texts for children (such as trade books, school texts, and periodicals). These criteria do not represent all possible elements of nonfiction and/or non-narrative texts. Developing knowledge about these kinds of texts often requires teachers to do some research, locating different texts from various disciplines and noting what they contain. These searches can be tailored to the projects and investigations children are conducting, finding alternative examples to fit the children's aims and the information they are trying to acquire.

Content

Before providing or reading nonfiction texts with children, teachers will want to be familiar with their content. Is the *information* they contain correct? This doesn't mean eliminating books that contain erroneous information or that vary from a single viewpoint. It may mean, however, that as we read with children, we use questioning to highlight differing views or facts across texts. It may mean deciding that a certain type of text does not contain the needed information (as in the bee investigation in chapter 4). This may lead readers to rely less on some texts and locate more useful ones. It may mean introducing genres that add detail to a reader's knowledge (as in Jack's insect investigation). On the other hand, the text may contain so much information that a child who comes to it with little or no prior knowledge would not be able to make use of it.

Finally, the vocabulary used in various types of nonfiction texts can take children beyond the everyday words that are used in a discipline (Martin, 1993). For example, does the book leave children with general terms that do not reflect accurate content? (Can every insect be classified as a "bug"?) Young children love technical vocabulary—look at the number of dinosaur names many kindergartners can reel off! Vocabulary should not be restricted to nouns or names, however. Processes and activities (such as "preserving" fossils) should appear in nonfiction texts.

The cognition of young children is based on perception and concreteness; preschoolers, for example, are much more apt to define something by describing what to do with it or by telling an anecdote from their own experience than by giving an objective definition (Berger, 1986). Thus, the technical vocabulary in non-

Table 5.1. Some Questions to Ask about
Nonfiction and Non-narrative Texts

CONTENT
- Is the information correct?
- If not, what clues suggest that the information is inaccurate, or that it might be fictive?
- Is the genre appropriate to the purpose or area of inquiry (e.g., a nonfiction narrative for biography, a classification or research report for science)?
- Who would best make use of the text?
  - Would a child who knows little or nothing about the topic be able to make use of the text?
  - Would a child need a great deal of prior knowledge in order to gain from the text?
  - Would a child who has considerable prior knowledge about the topic be able to add detail to this knowledge?

TEXT ORGANIZATION
- Is the text ordered or does it appear to be unordered?
- Does the text contain chapters? If so, how are they organized?
  - By topic?
  - By types?
  - By the steps of a process, as in a *how* explanation?
  - By sequenced topics (e.g., the development of allergic reactions)?
- What kind of mental picture does the text help children to develop using the information? A classification? A *how* explanation?
- Does the text essentially comprise a list?
- Is the text simply a list of descriptions (e.g., of a particular kind of insect)?
- Are the descriptions broken down into logical categories (e.g., physical characteristics, habitat, diet)?
- Does the text follow a natural or scientific process but using narrative devices (e.g., characters and a plot)?
- Does the text correspond to a conventional genre?
- Does the text use the appropriate point of view for its genre (e.g., are first-person pronouns used for *how* descriptions? Does an information text about bees refer to "my honeybee"?)?
- Are diagrams labeled with appropriate technical terms?
- Do labeled diagrams or illustrations correspond to the text on that page so that the text becomes more comprehensible?

Table 5.1. *(continued)*

ILLUSTRATIONS
- Are the illustrations actually the subject of the text?
- Alternatively, do the illustrations primarily augment and add to the text?
- Are the illustrations appropriate to the genre and the area of inquiry (e.g., are data tables appropriately constructed or do they look more like mind maps)?
- Do graphic devices (e.g., histograms, bar graphs) appropriately characterize different types of data?

---

fiction texts needs to be sufficiently illustrated and defined so that children can understand it. Often, this will be accomplished through illustrations as well as text. In this case, the term should appear adjacent to the illustration (not two pages away) so that children can readily make an accurate connection.

A final aspect of content also relates to the function, or purpose, of a text. What does it aim to do? How many functions does it undertake? Usually, as we've seen, text does more than one thing. Does a letter contain a personal narrative? Does a classification explain? A further issue is whether or not the genre choice or choices serve the primary purpose of the text. This doesn't simply mean deciding whether or not the text follows a conventional form; the question is whether or not it works. In this light, is the genre an appropriate one? This is a central choice for composers, and one that can be made innovatively. Children's reading should expose them to a variety of traditional and innovative genre choices, making this knowledge conscious so that readers can understand the choices that other writers have made. This also relates to the features, or compositional elements, of different kinds of texts.

Text Features

Teachers also need to determine whether a text conveys information in a form that is appropriate to that subject area. This includes the organizational features of the written text as well as the illustrations. Such features include topic organization: Does the organization make sense to readers? Does the text contain the features of the conventional genres used in that area of inquiry? If not, how does it vary? Does it combine features of classification and explanation? In addition, the text should make use of the correct point of view for the genre. An informational text about frogs, for example, does not typically focus on "my frog," but on "frogs" in general. As a result, first-person references ("I" and "we") are less frequent than third-person references ("it" and "they"). Chapter 3 details principal text features of various conventional and child-created composing choices (genres).

School texts and children's nonfiction books do not always follow the organization of conventional texts in a genre. For example, many nonfiction children's books are organized deductively. In other words, general information is given first, followed by more specific information or examples. In contrast, some conventional science texts, such as field guides, are organized inductively with specific observational information leading to classification (Owens, 1999). This organization may be more accessible to young children, who learn concretely. These kinds of conventional texts may actually be easier for children to use for many purposes. To use deductively organized texts, children have to first locate the general, and perhaps more abstract, information and follow it to the specific information. This may not reflect their thinking processes. Focused reading with children can help them to first locate the specific information they need and then use the text more effectively in ways that make sense for their purposes.

Again, all examples need not be good examples. Texts that conflict with expectations allow readers to apply their knowledge of text features to an evaluation of their reading materials. If too much information is conveyed in an illogical format, would only a well-informed reader find it accessible? These readers have already developed a store of information and a mental organization for it. They can approach the text more selectively. Not all texts fit all readers.

Illustrations

Acquainting children with genre also focuses on noticing the use of appropriate illustrations and visual organizers, such as charts, data tables, flow charts, and diagrams (Moline, 1995). For example, while webs may allow children to trace the links they are making between points as they read, or are read to, they are not usually a part of conventional science genres (Shepardson and Britsch, 2001). The next sections describe some of the distinctive visual elements appropriate to the texts in several areas of inquiry.

Science Texts.

In science texts, taxonomies visually illustrate classifications via tree diagrams branching out from the largest category at the top to the next smaller sets (Martin, 1993). For example, children might separate some orders of mammals such as rodents, bats, primates, and insectivores (e.g., moles, hedgehogs, shrews). Then, for example, rodents might be divided into beavers, guinea pigs, mice, squirrels, and so on (Vaughn, 1978, pp. 39–41). Children's taxonomies might distinguish these kinds of groupings within mammals even if they do not represent the full scientific classifications. They still trace the relationships between types of organisms. This will undergird a child's classification (as in Chapter 4, for instance).

In science research reports, data tables show numerical or descriptive findings that are organized by row and column. A data table is a kind of chart (Harlan, 1992). It may, for example, list different types of rock down one side (row). A set of characteristics would appear in headings across the top (column). The cells inside the table would describe that characteristic for each type of rock. Data tables also group items based on two variables. For example, a set of rubber-band thicknesses may be shown horizontally across the top of the matrix while the vertical axis lists pitch variations. The cells would record whether each rubber band produced that pitch. Another kind of graphic often found in the research report of an experiment is a detailed drawing of the apparatus as part of the procedure, or method, section. Composition (i.e., part-whole relationships, such as the parts of a fly) is often shown with written descriptions that accompany labeled diagrams (Martin, 1993). Teachers can draw children's attention to these visual elements and consider whether the graphics reflect the written text; whether they do not, in fact, relate to anything being addressed by the adjacent written text; or whether the illustrations themselves are actually the subject addressed by the text.

Social Studies Texts.

Like science texts, geographies use language to observe, to "order the experiential world" and to explain it (Wignell, Martin, and Eggins, 1993, p. 137). They do this through description, classification, and explanation mirrored by the visual devices in the texts. Here again, taxonomies may show hierarchies or classifications (e.g., climate types). Social studies texts that are nonfiction narratives (e.g., stories from the history of a country) may highlight significant aspects of the narrative with maps of various kinds, detailed and captioned drawings of the inventions from various eras, reproductions of historical documents, portraits of historical figures, and paintings or photographs of crucial scenes, locations, and buildings. If these are presented only through drawings (not photographs), readers may question the time frame of the text, leading to research about whether the structures still exist or have changed dramatically, or whether events occurred so long ago that they could not be recorded by photography.

Biographies, too, may contain portraits, reproductions of documents written by the subject, photographs or drawings of events in which the subject participated, or products that the subject invented. Readers can examine these to see how closely they link with the written text or a timeline chronicling life events. Readers can also search the illustrations for details not noted in the written text or evaluate the appropriateness of the illustration choices, justifying the inclusion of other graphics that more effectively illuminate the subject's life.

Mathematical Texts.

Mathematical texts often contain *how* and *why* explanations followed by the equations that express those concepts. As symbolic statements, equations model and display real world relationships. Drawings, tables, graphs, and words can also be used to represent these relationships (American Association for the Advancement of Science, 1990). Expository texts that use mathematics to describe and explain how the world works contain illustrations suitable to the information being given. They may use graphs such as histograms to show distributions. For example, the horizontal scale may show income in thousands of dollars while blocks of differently sized areas represent the number of families with each income. While histograms represent quantities by area, bar graphs represent quantities by the height of the column (Freedman, Pisani, and Purves, 1978). Finally, scales with vertical and horizontal axes are used to relate two kinds of information (such as the height and weight of a group of people). These often report the results of surveys (Freedman, Pisani, and Purves, 1978).

Readers may challenge the workability of these tools to describe certain results or their suitability to characterize different types of data, necessitating new choices (Whitin and Whitin, 1998). This kind of critical literacy can begin early, helping readers to detect fallacies and faulty presentations of information that skew facts.

Focused Reading

Based on what teachers know about the construction of nonfiction and non-narrative texts, they can help to point out key elements of different genres in reading interactions with children. This kind of discussion differs from content questions about the information in a text because it focuses on how the text is organized and how other texts of this type are set up. The following sections describe ways of using focused reading to work with various types of texts.

Lists and Descriptions

Suppose you are working with a book for preschoolers or kindergartners that lists, illustrates, and describes the jobs of various community helpers, each on a separate page but in no particular order. Here, focused reading might become a kind of game.

This kind of game helps very young children use non-narrative texts to look up things they want to know. Perhaps they'll find that the book actually classifies the community helpers in some way, and then breaks down the various aspects of their jobs. Or perhaps they'll find that the list is random. This is critical literacy for young children, enabling them to evaluate their reading. The game also provides a reading strategy for particular kinds of books; it's a short jump from here to the use of children's dictionaries, for example. Or encyclopedias. Or field guides.

Organize the Book

If an informational picture book essentially comprises a random list of objects or people, play a game instead of simply reading each page of the book.

- Look through the book to find the bold headings, or labels, on each page.
- Ask the group which community helper they would like to find out about first.
- Locate that page by the heading, or using the table of contents if one is included.
- Point out the pictures on that page and talk about what readers can learn about that helper from each illustration.
- Read the adjacent text with the children. Does it correspond to the illustration or add to the illustration?
- Choose another helper whose work might be related to that of the first. Does that page follow the first in a logical order?
- Repeat the reading procedure.
- Begin to compile the children's findings. Do they want to reorder the pages to make their own book? Can they think of other community helpers whose work is much like another's in some way or who work with another helper?

To follow up the reading game, ask the children to tell you what they have learned about different community helpers from the book—don't simply recapitulate it yourself. Record the children's ideas on chart paper. Talk about other questions the children have about particular helpers. If the book doesn't provide that information, this can spur further reading together in other books found on a library visit, located on a website, or obtained by talking with classroom visitors. As this investigation continues and the children gather information, reread the chart paper findings and questions. What kinds of new information have they obtained? Which of the children's questions have been answered? Which remain? Which are now irrelevant and can be replaced with more focused questions?

Expository Texts

Suppose that in the course of an investigation in a primary grade classroom, the children have located a book that provides descriptions of various kinds of bees and explains what happens when a bee stings a human. Go beyond simply reading through each section of the book and question it instead.

By focusing the reading of expository texts on questions, children prepare to use books selectively in a literature search. Good researchers usually collect information that goes beyond their immediate or initial questions (Flower, 1990). Reading then becomes a process through which researchers create and expand their mental pictures of what they know, and begin to discern what they don't know. Focused reading may introduce readers to new thinking processes and stimulate questioning that moves research forward. It may also provide ways of relating to text that transfer to other projects, other subject matter, and other situations.

Question the Book

When the children in a primary classroom have designed some of the questions that will focus an investigation (e.g., about bees), focus their reading through further questioning based on the subject of the investigation and on the gaps in their knowledge.

One question might be "Are all bees the same?" Locate several relevant books and begin to diagram the answers in order to compare them for similarities and differences. This may result in a concept list or a classification.

A next question might be "Can all bee stings make you sick?" Though it's a yes/no question, readers might look for a *why* explanation to fully answer it. Locate several books that should address this question. Do the books discuss allergies to bee stings? If so, how? Do they describe the process of a bee sting (a *how* explanation) and some possible reactions or do they actually explain something about why bee stings cause adverse reactions (a *why* explanation)?

If a book addresses bee stings, has the passage answered the readers' question specifically enough? The children may decide that the book isn't useful for their purposes. Now a library or web search can become more focused and critical.

Are some sources more complete than others? Do certain types of books or certain authors seem to be more reliable than others? Are readers able to recognize an author who is an authority on the topic?

Classifications

Imagine a nonfiction children's text about fish. It describes and classifies different freshwater and saltwater fish, erroneously including in this set mammals such as whales, dolphins, and porpoises. Check the accuracy of the book by using the appropriate genre.

As you read with the children, begin to diagram the classification that results (Martin, 1993). Read in a focused way, perhaps using a tree diagram as you select descriptions and contrast them. Begin by reading one of the descriptions for a freshwater fish: Which creature is the author telling us about here (i.e., the name of the creature)? What kinds of detail does the description include? What kind of creature does the book say this is (i.e., begin to create groupings beyond specific names for each creature).

Move to another freshwater fish description: "How is this next description like the first one? Should we group it with the first fish? Should we call this a category? What should we name it?"

Now find a contrasting entry for a freshwater fish. "Which piece of information in the description contrasts with the earlier ones? Do we need another category?"

Then turn to the mammals. Repeat the process to find regularities that will solidly differentiate the categories.

You may finish with a classification that subsumes whales, dolphins, and porpoises under the category of "saltwater fish," according to the inaccurate text. Alternatively, the children may decide that three categories are needed. Pursue either conclusion by asking: "How do we know that's right?" and "How can we check?"

If the children have simply diagrammed the text, without question, how do they know the book is right?

Perhaps you'll rewrite the book together, or write your own based on correct information that the children research and their accurate classification. Then re-evaluate the original text: what have we learned? Which aspects of the book are useful? Which are not? What will we watch for next time we read a book like this?

Fictional Truth

Next, read a fictional narrative. Imagine that it's a story about a porpoise that has gotten lost and ended up in a pond behind a child's house. The porpoise likes it there because the child feeds it peanut butter and jelly sandwiches. But because both the child and the porpoise are lonely, the child begins to talk to the porpoise and it learns to speak. The child learns to understand porpoise utterances. They learn about friendship from each other. One day, the child tries to swim with the porpoise but, being a poor swimmer, gets into trouble. The porpoise rescues the child. They learn that, along with the ability to adapt to each other in significant ways, friends respect each other's differences and strengths.

The difference between a novelist and a historian, then, lies in the roles they intentionally assume (Banfield, 1982). Unlike a piece of nonfiction, fiction creates its own truth:

> [T]he fictional narrative statement is immune to judgments of truth or falsity; in fiction, they are suspended. It is inappropriate to say that a fictional statement is false. Rather it creates by fiat a fictional reality which can only be taken as fictionally true (Banfield, 1982, p. 258).

Fictional narratives often convey accurate information via fictional devices. In fact, the language in some pieces of fiction may not sound very fictional. As children begin to read critically, they can be on the lookout for fact in fiction. Teachers also need to be on the lookout for fictional texts that may seem to convey factual information but don't! Focused reading helps children to recognize a classification or a research report and differentiate it from fictional narrative. This helps them to assume a different stance, not only that of a storywriter.

Fiction Can't Be False

From the nonfiction classification they've read previously, the children have learned that porpoises live in oceans and can't survive in a pond. Many other fallacies are present in the story as well. Factually, however, it's known that porpoises and dolphins use sounds to communicate within a school.

Is the story wrong?

In terms of facts about porpoises, yes. But not entirely.

Should it be changed as we amended the nonfiction text?

No. Fiction writers, unlike science writers, create imaginary scenes. This means they get to decide what is true and what is false in that scene. They mean to create fantasy in order to say something that is true. This story shows how one writer did that.

By contrasting fiction with nonfiction, children can see for themselves that stories are "pretend" in many ways. But the story about the porpoise also conveys an essential truth, not only about human relationships but also about the relationship between humans and animals. This is a characteristic of both fiction and nonfiction. In this sense, fiction *is* true, for the writer and (the writer hopes) for the reader as well. If well done, it draws us in, makes us feel something for the characters, and learn something about ourselves. This is not generally the purpose of non-narrative genres, although rhetorical pieces, such as arguments, do aim to make the reader react, certainly intellectually and often emotionally. (Supposedly, these are based on fact, but sometimes they're not, or the facts are slanted and only selectively included.) Nonfiction narrative, such as biography, can assume many of the same functions as fiction, and have the same effects on the reader (see Chapter 3). The difference is that the writer comes to it from a different stance, intending the events illustrated to be accurate— usually. Unconventional biographies exist in which fictional characters are included. The value and believability of this technique in constructing biography has been questioned. Still, the intention of the writer is not to change historical fact but to draw the reader into the subject's story (Carvajal, 1999).

Children can engage in this kind of informed, critical reading. Without the ability to distinguish between the genres they read, children may confuse erroneous information with fact. As they write, they may commingle fictional devices and non-narrative purposes. Both fictional and factual texts require responsible handling, but factual texts require a reader and writer responsibility that involves constructive skepticism. For example, in a project described by David and Phyllis Whitin (1998), fourth graders who conducted bird observations decided to investigate the reduction of tanager habitats due to forest cutting. To do this, they first created diagrams that modeled a forest cut into smaller and smaller squares. The children challenged this model, some objecting that most forest cutting probably happens much less systematically and geometrically. Next, they constructed alternative models and concluded that the impact of forest cutting upon tanagers probably increases over time. They surveyed habitat features and pointed out questions that were not posed in the survey. This critical approach invited the children to recognize underlying assumptions and question them. Their choices changed the nonfiction devices they used, and can change children's views of reading visual and verbal text:

> As skeptics the children also began to see that *how* a set of data is graphed both conceals and reveals information. Graphs are nonfiction texts; when children construct these graphical texts, they need to be aware of how the choices they make influence the way an audience reads and interprets the text (Whitin and Whitin, 1998, p. 127).

These children took a stance toward investigation and the way that texts represent what we know. Teachers can promote an atmosphere in which this sort of thought can occur by using questions that stimulate and structure inquiry by children. Reading, like composing, becomes a way of participating in the world and an awareness of the power of visual and written literacy.

Reading and Composing

Reading is a part of composing because it both inspires and reflects children's own composing choices. As we focus children's reading, they hear the kinds of questions they can also ask as they compose and read their own pieces. Reading their own work is a prelude to revision because they can begin to see

- ♦ what's missing
- ♦ what requires more detail
- ♦ what's disorganized
- ♦ what's irrelevant
- ♦ what's in an authentic voice.

Composers can also read their work with the teacher or with peers. An audience can respond as would a reader in that area of inquiry—reading a research report as a scientist would, or listening to an argument for wetland conservation as an animal advocate would (Martin, 1993). Some composers need this kind of response from others first, then they turn to more solitary reading and revision. Others keep their work private for some time, until they're satisfied with it themselves; only then do they offer it to an audience.

As with the focused reading of trade books, questioning can surround the reading of children's self-produced texts. For example, the following object description resulted from a kindergartner's examination of a fossil with a hand lens. The description in Figure 5.1a is visual, detailed by the child's written labels, shown in Figure 5.1b. The composer can read and/or describe the pages. Some of the kinds of questions suggested in Table 5.2 might respond by making use of the text features of object descriptions.

A teacher wouldn't necessarily want to discuss all of these questions at the same time, but might start with one or two of the features of an object description, based on what the child has included. Oral responses can be recorded by the teacher and then read again as a basis for going on to a new investigation or another composing choice. Although this may begin as teacher-directed talk, the aim over time is for these to become the questions that composers ask themselves.

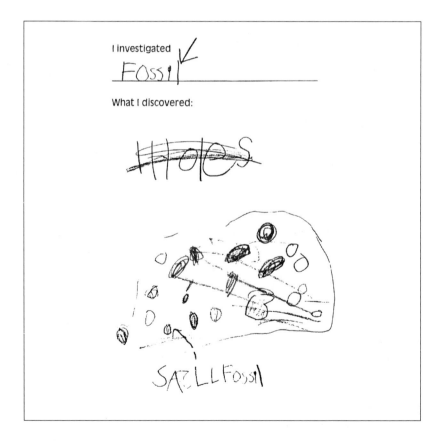

Figure 5.1a A child's visual description of fossils.

Table 5.2 Focused Reading of an Object Description

TEXT FEATURES	FOCUS QUESTIONS
Details as arranged in space	Let's look at each part. What were they? Written text in Figure 5.1b: "Holes, designs, shape, lines, broken off." Were the holes everywhere on the fossil? Were they different sizes? (Note the child's drawing.)
	Where were the lines? Were they on top of or across the holes? Did the lines curve or were they straight? What kind of design did the lines make? (Based on drawing.)
	How was the fossil shaped? Was it like the shape of anything else you know? Written text in Figure 5.1a: "shell fossil."
	What other kinds of shapes do we find? Coral shapes? Animal shapes? Insect shapes (i.e., from organisms such as trilobites, brachiopods, or coral)?
Observer in a single spot	Did you look at it from different directions? How did you look at it first? Then where did you move the hand lens?
	How did it look different from the other side?
Detail expressed	What did the shape look like? What different kinds of designs were there? Teeth? Bones? Shells?
Precise vocabulary	What technical words can we use to tell about what we observed? **Paleontologists** study fossils. The rock around the fossil is the **matrix**. Some of the remains of a plant or animal are **preserved** as fossils. The **exoskeletons** of **invertebrates** are often preserved. Paleontologists often make a **mold** of the fossil in order to study a **specimen**.

Figure 5.1b A child's written description of fossils.

The teacher might follow up with a new experience in which the composer molds clay inside a shell, the way paleontologists work. The teacher might suggest various kinds of *how* explanations by asking these questions:

- Can we find out how the fossil was made?
- How do paleontologists find fossils?
- What made the holes?
- What made the shapes?
- Why does it look like it's broken off?

Figure 5.2 shows a child's drawn-written response to an examination of owl pellets. In contrast to Figures 5.1a and 5.1b, Figure 5.2 is an activity description instead of an object description. The composer has written, "We look at pellets and we look for mice bones." While the written language functions as an activity description, the drawing (in pencil and brown marker) accurately conveys the opaque quality of the owl pellets. As the child "reads" both words and drawing, the teacher might think about the text features of a research report. From this point of view, the composer's written language actually commingles an aim and a general procedure. The teacher might focus this reading as suggested in Table 5.3.

This questioning is based on the child's composing, but it also suggests new experience that will guide further composing (e.g., Martin, 1993). Questioning can also point out different ways of representing the same experience using different genres. Teachers can note the ways in which children's compositions vary (across cases), the ways in which they change over time (within cases), as well as the understandings that different composers can articulate best through oral language or drawing instead of writing.

Table 5.3 Focused Reading of an Activity Description

TEXT FEATURES	FOCUSED READING
Aim	"We look at pellets and . . .
Procedure	". . . we look for mice bones."
	How did we look for them? What tools did we use? What did we use in order to see more closely?
Results	What did we find?
	What did it look like through the hand lens? (Refer to the child's drawing in pencil and brown marker, figure 5.2.)
	Did we find anything other than bones? Which parts of the mouse did we find? How can we tell?
Conclusion	What did we learn about what owls eat? What does this tell us about how owls digest their food?
	So, why do owl pellets exist?

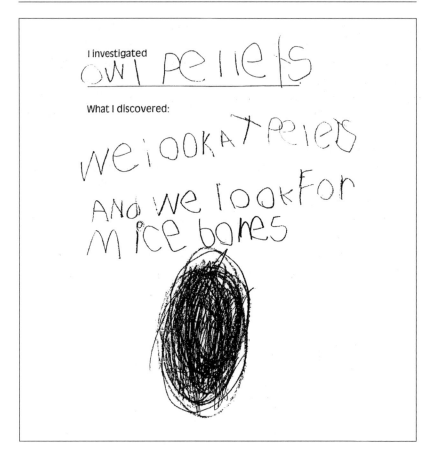

Figure 5.2 An activity description from an examination of owl pellets.

Toward Nonfiction Creativity

Through focused reading, child composers can develop an awareness of the features that are both usual and unusual for different genres. This doesn't prohibit the creative use of literary tools in unconventional ways; in fact, it leads to a kind of nonfiction creativity in which children take alternative viewpoints, construct better ways of investigating, and represent knowledge in new ways. Writers engage in this kind of creativity with awareness, not haphazardly or because they possess only one set of tools for a variety of tasks.

Informed readers, too, can appreciate variations and the effects they have. They can recognize which purposes call for certain conventions, and how those conventions can be expressed more originally through tools that composers control. Informed readers appreciate the writing styles of composers who purposefully vary textual elements to offer something of themselves, a dimension of composing that teachers can open up through the reading of non-fiction and non-narrative texts.

Chapter 6

Assessment as a Nonjudgmental Process

Following and Fostering Change

All of our interactions with children as they create nonfiction compositions are really assessments. We are constantly watching to see what each child notices and represents graphically and in writing, in play and talk. We need ways of recording and compiling what we are learning about children's responses so we can see what to offer next. Vygotsky (1978) distinguished two levels, or zones, of development: the actual and the proximal. The zone of actual development indicates what the child can do alone, without interaction with others. The zone of proximal development indicates what the child can do with the assistance of others. It defines functions that are in the process of maturing, not those that have already matured. We address our teaching to that zone:

> [L]earning which is oriented toward developmental levels that have already been reached is ineffective from the viewpoint of a child's overall development. It does not aim for a new stage of the developmental process but rather lags behind the process (Vygotsky, 1978, p. 89).

For Vygotsky, the only "good learning" is that which "is in advance of development" (1978, p. 89). Our teaching, then, helps children to move forward if it is *pitched* slightly beyond what's easy, what's quickly done, what's already mastered. Assessment helps us to determine that level for each child. To do this, we do not focus on children's factual knowledge alone. Maxine Greene cautions against equating the factual with the intellectual.

> We forget that such facts are only data; they are only fragmentary, uncompleted meanings, which need to be rounded into complete ideas. This work that can only be done by a free imagination full of intellectual possibilities (Greene, 2001, p. 2).

Children can engage in this imaginative work through nonfiction composition. It's this work that we aim both to energize and to follow with our assessments. We can see the child's present response not as "a static moment, but a mass of different combinations of past and present relations" (Holquist, 1990). Teachers interact not just with what is present but also with what is unarticulated, unrealized—the zone of proximal development.

This means that the information teachers have about conventional genres should be used not as curricular method but to guide the kind of exploration Maxine Greene describes. Teachers apply the knowledge base they've developed to the combination of situations, purposes, and choices moments that coalesce as children develop their composing.

Of course, all children do not move forward in a lockstep way. The development of written language is an organized process, but it's differently organized for each child (Vygotsky, 1978). At first, as Vygotsky said, meaning arises from action. Action determines the function of print, talk, and drawing. Gradually, the ratio flips. Children use talk, play, drawing, and writing for purposes that are both old and new at the same time—purposes that the children can write themselves into in much the same way that adult writers follow the line of their own interests to develop new responses and new purposes. The thinking processes and the action underlying this use of genre arise from moments, from activity, instead of being presented as isolated formats or templates. Teaching is not based on gimmicks that compel children to fake a need and to respond using teacher-provided formulae.

Real opportunities for nonfiction composing will also frequently motivate and reveal capacities not accessed in story writing. This reveals a new and broader picture of the child's literacy capacities. A child may have a great deal of knowledge about lists, for example, and may encode this non-narrative genre through word-initial consonants while writing stories in linear mock writing (e.g., Zecker, 1999).

Assessment of these capacities does not mean pitting them against a standard that the child either meets or misses. Instead, assessment guides the development of responsive teaching by noting the different approaches that children take to composing over time—the organized but individual development of a child's use of genre. In this sense, assessment is a nonjudgmental process, valuing and making use of the fact that there are many lines of development. Teachers can then continue to expand the contexts and the tools that enable children to respond in more varied and more complex ways.

What about Standards?

"What I've been taught to construct," Winston Weathers has lamented, "is the well-made box." He summed up his training in composition in this way:

> I have been taught to put "what I have to say" into a container that is always remarkably the same, that—in spite of varying decorations—keeps to a basically conventional form: a solid bottom, four upright sides, a fine-fitting lid. . . . And I begin to wonder if there isn't somewhere a round box or oval box or tubular box, if somewhere there isn't some sort of a container . . . that will be more suitable perhaps to my own mental processes (Weathers, 1980, pp. 1–2).

The irony is that child composers start out by doing just this. Because nonfiction composing is a "human gesture of response" (Newkirk, 2000, p. 41), inherently variable and multifunctional, the notion of standardized measures of composing competence is a contradictory one. A standardized measure, to be valid, would first have to resolve the conflict implied by the use of an instrument that seeks uniformity as an assessment of variation.

Still, composers do need knowledge of composing conventions to help shape their writing. This suggests that one aim of teaching should be to familiarize student writers with the options in areas such as vocabulary, sentence forms, paragraph types, and organization (Weathers, 1980). To simply assess the mechanics of a piece of nonfiction, however, won't get at what makes it remarkable.

"I don't categorize as I go along," says the novelist Maxine Hong Kingston. "I break through categories" (Schroeder, 1998, p. 216). This requires control of, rather than restriction by, form. The composer has to "choose the technique, which, for one thing, presupposes familiarity with all the possibilities" (Moffett, 1968, p. 153).

What, then, is the real purpose for the assessment of children's composing? Is it to evaluate variation from a norm (raising the specter of a deficit view)? Or is it to constantly offer new contexts and tools that do not reduce the act of responsive composing to an enforcement of uniformity (Newkirk, 2000, p. 41)? Teachers are in a prime position to assess children's composing skills: they see children using language all day and, with an awareness of the kinds of variation they might see and an openness to others, they can detect and react to all kinds of subtleties. On this view, assessment should characterize composing both on its own creative and developmental terms and in relation to a range of possible options "already established in the language" (Weathers, 1980, p. 5). Effective assessment can also enable teachers to relate this informed and regular observation to the effectiveness of methods and materials.

The previous chapters in this book have suggested ways in which teachers can interact with children during the moments, or scenes, that guide their exploration of nonfiction composition in the classroom. How does a child's composing evolve? When does a teacher need to vary purpose and suggest new forms for a particular composer? Which activities motivate the richest composition for different composers? Which activities motivate nothing? How can we keep track of this over time? The next sections suggest some answers.

Beginning

Chapter 2 suggests a diagnostic assessment task based on Zecker's 1999 study of young children's knowledge about genre (see "Observation as Assessment," Zecker, 1999). As teachers find moments to engage in this kind of activity with individuals or small groups of children, they begin to compile findings, much as an anthropologist would do. This formulates a picture of how children use oral language as well as drawing and written language.

Table 6.1 begins by suggesting a chart of the language functions that might be observed in a small group of composers. These descriptions or identifications need not be limited to one genre, nor should they only include conventional genres. They should simply record the various ways in which a child responds through composing. Then teachers can ask themselves further questions: What is the *child* doing by means of this composing? Is this explanation done by narration? Is this a warning given by labeling (as in Chapter 2)? This picture of the functions for children's composing may be combined with the type of assessment suggested in Chapter 2 (see Table 2.1).

Such an assessment can also highlight patterns and regularities. When several children are currently focusing on similar purposes, further small-group activity can be designed. Based on recurring composing functions and a focus on science content, the group illustrated in Table 6.1 might next focus on classifications and/or *how* or *why* explanations through extended science experiences.

Table 6.1. Assessing Composing Functions

COMPOSING FUNCTION	WHAT WOULD WE CALL IT?
Jack: Describes insect characteristics, sorts insects, and generalizes	Drawing/diagram Classification Concept list
Eric: Narrates natural process of leaf decomposition	*How*-explanation Narrative Labeled process diagram
Sam: Explains plant growth	*Why*-explanation with composition diagram Cause-effect statement Activity description *How*-explanation
Nicholas: Classifies crystals by characteristics	Classification Labeled diagrams

Another way of looking at the various familiar forms that children are choosing for various composing purposes is suggested in Table 6.2. Composers differentially match form with function. For example, the group of third graders described in Chapter 4 chose five different forms (lists, interviews, webs, letters, research reports) and used each for various functions. Table 6.2 records these forms in the left column and the various functions performed by each form in the right column. This highlights the fact that written composing choices are functions as well as forms. It also allows teachers to see what the children are working with, and to make curricular judgments on this basis.

Continuing

To record the trajectory of a child's composing choices over time, we might construct a chart such as the one shown in Table 6.3. Each time a new type of response appears, or a new topic for a response, we record it. This way, we can see what's developing and how the child's interest is shifting. In other words, how is the composing embedded in the child's activity? Suppose Annie initially focuses on telling stories through object descriptions. This

Table 6.2. Assessing Form and Function

FORM	FUNCTION
List	Object description Concept list *How*-explanation
Interview	Label *Why*-explanation
Web	Classification of concepts
Letter	Concept list *How*-explanation Narrative
Research report	Classification
	Report including focal statement Three foci organized by paragraph Practical recommendations

occurs while she is looking at books in the library corner. Then she moves to oral *how* explanations during activity at a learning center or during a project. Based on the child's freeplay activity, which focuses on the woodworking center, the teacher may invite a *how* explanation about the boat she's just built. This may be dictated, because Annie isn't writing yet, and read later during "story time" (renamed "reading time") as the boat itself is shared.

Next, we might observe that this composer's purpose shifts to include a *how* explanation of a construction project that a neighbor is starting. This time, the composer requests a dictation and adds oral nonfiction narrative to her way of constructing *how* explanations. Perhaps dictation is necessary for this language

Table 6.3. A Developmental Genre Assessment

Child's name: Annie

DATES	GENRES	GRAPHIC MEDIUM	ORAL LANGUAGE
9/26 9/29 9/30	Story as object description based on book in library corner	Drawing	Describes characters
10/15	*How*-explanation of boatbuilding at woodworking center		Lists materials; tells steps
10/18	*How*-explanation of boatbuilding at reading time	Teacher-suggested dictation: lists materials; tells steps; narrates neighbor's boatbuilding	Oral reading in own words
11/1	*How*-explanation of fence building at writing table	Diagram and child-requested dictation: lists materials; tells steps; labels diagram at reading time	Oral reading

function; Annie has not yet independently used written language at all. She next adds diagrams to this set of features of her *how* explanations. A whole unit could result from this set of scenes— boats, construction, water, or perhaps all three, based on the connections the children are forming.

This assessment reveals that Annie is constantly elaborating her *how* explanations by adding features, some conventional and others dictated by her own developing capacities. Looking at Table 6.3, we can see that she carries out her composing activity across different settings. This suggests that time needs to be made available for child-selected writing tasks throughout the day. We can also see that she is adding graphic representation of her purposes to her oral language functions. She requests a dictation after the teacher has suggested this; perhaps this works as a way of elaborating her *how* explanations. She then maintains this familiar composing choice, which frees her to work on new media and new features. Her cognitive energy can now be devoted to this.

This sort of developmental genre assessment can then be expanded to address a group of children, as in Table 6.4. This reveals patterns that are developing across the group of children. It also highlights the gaps and suggests directions for future activity. The group shown in Table 6.2 is familiar with fictional narrative. While we certainly don't want to eliminate stories, the children are including more written language in their activity descriptions. We might want to focus on these for work on the phonics aspects of writing, such as sound-symbol connections or word analysis. Only one child has worked with *how* explanations, however—perhaps because the activity simply hasn't taken the others there yet. This might motivate a unit on construction. One composing aim might be to link the logical organization of personal activity descriptions with the step-by-step nature of more generalized *how* explanations.

As children's oral and written composing becomes more complex, teachers can look further into the use of text features. Both Tables 6.3 and 6.4 can be adapted to include more descriptive detail of individual development of the functions and text features of children's composing. While the information recorded can be based on the features of composing choices like those shown in Chapter 3, the assessment should not be limited to those items alone. In all cases, a close description of what the composer initiates and contributes to the composing is the most essential basis

Table 6.4. A Developmental Genre Assessment

	Annie	Jack	Sarah
Fictional narrative	9/26, 9/29, 9/30: draw and talk	9/6: Oral retelling from trade book	9/15: Oral + dramatized
How-explanation	10/15: oral 10/18: dictated 11/1: dictated		
Activity description	10/22: oral and invented spelling (word-initial consonants)	9/15: draw and talk 9/17: draw and dictated	9/16: retold from drawing and labels

for further teaching. This focuses teaching on the child's use of the genre, not the teacher's.

Regular tape recording of literacy events can also highlight the children's way of enacting a genre much more clearly than observations on the spot. We hear details we'd missed in the actual situation, both in our own talk and in the children's. In fact, a tape recorder can become a familiar fixture at the writing table or during whole-group time. It isn't always possible to capture spontaneous activity, though, so a list of key words jotted down as soon as possible can work in a pinch. To take an example of oral composing, let's consider the kindergartner's oral account of plant growth shown in Chapter 1. This was a milestone, so we'd like to look at it more closely. In the best of all possible worlds, we'd audiotape it. Sam created his *why* explanation in response to a question about what would happen if we took a leaf off the tree and brought it inside. The question, though, had sprung from his idea about bringing a leaf inside to watch it turn green. Sam decided this wouldn't work and began his explanation by answering the question as succinctly as possible. Here's the core of the *why* explanation, missing a step or two:

Cause the tree would be giving the leaf oxygen . . . cause see the tree would be giving the leaf food and then the leaf would just die!

He continued by virtually arguing for his own solution while addressing the class. He proved his idea to himself by summarizing with a cause-effect statement followed by an imagined, or hypothetical, activity description that would remedy the problem proposed by his cause-effect statement:

> If we pick the leaf off the tree this spring then it will just <u>die</u>. So we have to go out to the tree and we have to <u>look</u> at the leaf so—if we're gonna do this <u>really big</u> we're gonna have to bring a whole tree to the classroom . . . and do you think that would be easy? NO!

He finished with a *how* explanation, chronicling how he believed trees obtain nourishment. As he did, he pointed to the large diagram the teacher had provided:

> The food comes down here . . . and it goes underground and then it comes up into the tree (Britsch, 2001b, pp. 112–113).

Sam's version of a *why* explanation, which was what he was building, consisted of these parts:

♦ *Why* explanation
♦ Cause-effect statement
♦ Activity description
♦ *How* explanation

We could summarize as in Table 6.5, using Table 6.3 as a model:

Table 6.5

DATE	GENRE	GRAPHIC MEDIUM	ORAL LANGUAGE
10/15	Explanation of plant growth at group time		*Why*-explanation Cause-effect statement Activity description
		++++++ Drawing Labels (using word-initial consonants and dictation)	*How*-explanation ++++++ Composition diagram

A conventional explanation would name the event or focus and then elaborate cause and effect. For Sam, the focus of his explanation was probably a given based on the context. His own idea had actually motivated the explanation. The initial question had simply focused his thinking and pushed it a bit further. He elaborated with his own cause-effect statement, the activity description, and the *how* explanation with reference to his audience. He addressed the class (and himself) because he wanted them to understand his thinking. He also did this with reference to the visual text the teacher had provided: the diagram of the tree. That's pretty complex. He's done a great deal of logical thinking. He then transferred his concepts to paper by turning air, water, and light into labeled cartoon characters in order to detail these elements of his explanation and make them concrete. This is a composition diagram—actually, a perfectly appropriate device for a science writer to use. It's just that the content isn't scientifically conventional.

This was Sam's version of an explanation, carried out (a) through talk addressed to an audience, and (b) on paper. His approach may change during the next scene that suggests to him the need for explanation. We'd note this change. Over time, composers "normalize" the design of a text in response to the environment (Kress, 1999, p. 468). This assumes that child composers can derive their own purposes, that they can alter the forms they use according to purpose, and that time is necessary to this development. Most essentially, it assumes that creativity is normal (Kress, 1999).

Teachers assess change in order to understand what is usual and what is unusual for individual children. What looks like a regression, for example, may simply mean that the composer is working on something new, focusing attention on that new element and letting other aspects of the composing task fall by the wayside temporarily (see, for instance, Werner, 1948). Because assessment need to account for these shifts, the items assessed also change over time in accord with changes in the children's activity.

Performance Standards

If they serve as benchmarks or guidelines, performance standards can be used in a way that contributes to formative assessment. They should not limit or dictate the teacher's entire set of aims or outcomes because children's learning opens up possibilities that reach beyond minimum standards. One approach is to combine developmental assessments of the type illustrated here with assessment that accounts for the standards. This readily allows teachers to design and adjust instruction based on the children's own nonfiction activity. For example, one set of English language arts standards for the elementary school specifies that writing objectives include reports of information, responses to literature, narrative accounts (fictional or autobiographical), and narrative procedures. A narrative procedure:

- engages the reader by establishing a context, creating a persona, and otherwise developing reader interest;
- provides a guide to action that anticipates a reader's needs; creates expectations through predictable structures, e.g., headings; and provides transitions between steps;
- makes use of appropriate writing strategies such as creating a visual hierarchy and using white space and graphics as appropriate;
- includes relevant information;
- excludes extraneous information;
- anticipates problems, mistakes, and misunderstandings that might arise for the reader;
- provides a sense of closure to the writing (Board of Education of the City of New York, 1997, p. 39).

What narrative procedures do implies a structure, and this is quite similar to the *how* explanations children may be composing. None of the above criteria exclude those functions and features. *How* explanations certainly establish a context (e.g., by stating the goal), and use a predictable structure (e.g, a list of materials and steps), including only relevant information. Used as guidelines, standards may suggest new composing foci that could be introduced, keeping in mind, however, that the purpose of assessment is "not to pin down that a child has mastered this skill or that idea, but to provide a basis for helping learning" (Harlan, 1992, p. 172).

Beyond Charts

Although the assessments shown here are formative and generally descriptive (not quantitative), they come across as fairly reductive in comparison with rich descriptions of children's activity in context. Teachers make mental notes all the time about who's doing what and how. They're habitual hypothesizers about why and why not. They carry anecdotes in their heads about children's activity which they sometimes find time to write down and sometimes don't. This means that teachers possess a great deal of awareness, which they use from moment to moment as they respond to children's needs. Through this constant assessment, they develop mental pictures of each child, from which they work. Sometimes it's helpful to see what we know on paper. Here are some systematic ways to record these kinds of pictures.

Logs

One strategy is to compile a log containing dated samples of a child's composing that represent starting points, typical activities, milestones, and changes (Waters, Frantz, Rottmayer, Trickett, and Genishi, 1992). This can reveal patterns we haven't seen, details that contribute to (or conflict with) our mental picture of a composer. This can be particularly enlightening if a composer's activity is puzzling, seems to have stalled, or has suddenly begun to speed forward. At intervals, a paragraph can summarize the current picture of a composer's pathway, consolidating and solidifying a number of pieces of the puzzle. These paragraphs can be inserted into a log or compiled in a notebook or computer file that the teacher rereads and reviews whenever necessary, certainly each time a new paragraph is added. As a result, we may also see patterns across the activities of several composers. This approach to assessing composers' work in turn suggests assessment of teachers that guides their response to the children's learning about the purposes and shapes of texts. How can teachers assess themselves?

Teacher Assessment: Linking Content with Composing

As horizontal thinkers (Elkind, 1987), children are linking contexts all the time, not boxing them off. We want to encourage these linkages to avoid developing curricula that require composers to simply fit their writing into a mold. As Kress points out, a newer way of thinking about genre is that

. . . within a general awareness of the range of genres, of their shapes, their contexts, speakers and writers newly make the generic forms out of available resources. This is a much more "generative" notion of genre; not one where you learn the shapes of existing kinds of texts alone in order to replicate them, but where you learn what the shapes of these texts are, and you learn the generative rules of the constitution of generic form within the power-structures of a society (Kress, 1999, p. 468).

This, Kress continues, promotes constant change. So with our observations, recorded as logs, as anecdotes, and/or on charts, we aim to highlight the kind of generativity and creativity that Kress suggests. We might also develop some general questions to ask ourselves as we interact with composers so that we can promote these kinds of processes in classroom composing scenes. These questions might include the following:

+ What do the children's readings of their written and drawn compositions tell us?
+ What role do drawings play in composing?
+ What sort of complexity do we see in oral genres?
+ Are oral genres broader in function or features than graphic or written genres?
+ How does the children's composing relate to the situations or environments around them? What motivates the compositions?
+ What are the features of a composer's definition of a genre and what do they do?

Teachers are scavengers for ideas for new activity that will answer these kinds of questions about children's needs as well as questions based on their own need to create a classroom atmosphere that will lend itself to creativity, generativity, and continuity. To illustrate a kind of curricular assessment that might be helpful, let's take a hypothetical example. At the beginning of a school year, we might want to acquaint children with the environment around the school, noticing the kinds of informational print there and its various uses. With this aim in mind, we might create an activity based on an idea from a favorite source, such as *Young Children in Action* (Hohmann, Banet, and Weikart, 1979):

Scene: Neighborhood Walk.

Aims.

To learn to locate things in the immediate environment; to gain a sense of spatial relations; to observe print details and their function in the immediate environment; and to represent the knowledge gained.

Elements of Scene Creation.

"Take walks around the block where the school is located. Look at the school from different angles and vantage points and help children notice places and permanent objects which can be used to make the way . . . Take photographs of landmarks on these walks . . .

"Also encourage children to make their own pictures of things they've seen on such walks" (Hohmann, Banet, and Weikart, 1979, p. 259).

Based on this idea we might notice and read signs, plaques, print on vehicles, and street signs. Ask the children to select which photos should be taken based on the print they notice. In the children's oral, written, and drawn compositions, we might look for classifications, nonfiction narratives, activity descriptions, and object descriptions. These may be elaborated in the classroom.

Key Concepts to Develop.

These could include the following, for example:
- Signs on buildings, beside buildings, and on streets give us information, direction, and rules to follow.
- Signs identify buildings.
- Plaques give us information and historical details.
- Lettering tells us about a vehicle's purpose.
- Colors and lettering identify mailboxes, fire hydrants, traffic signs, and vehicles.

Possible Follow-up Scenes.

- Sequencing or sorting photographs chronologically or by print functions

- Researching other objects, locations, or plants the children notice
- Compiling compositions into a class book
- Creating dramatic play centers that incorporate types of print observed
- Noting familiar and new informational print on subsequent field trips, around the school, and at home

Possible Composition Outcomes.

- Response types to watch for and suggest: classifications, nonfiction narratives, activity descriptions, object descriptions
- Use of appropriate vocabulary to name signs, plaques, and so on
- Reading of print and noting of appropriate function for this print in the environment

As we carry out this activity with the children, we can engage in the kinds of reflective tasks shown in Table 6.6 to assess planning and implementation. This matrix can be used to focus on individual or group activity as dictated by ongoing composing and experience.

This approach to assessment reflects general principles of active learning, continuity, teacher aims, and the children's role in directing activity. Over time, comparing one assessment with the next helps to assure continuity in content and composing outcomes. This links context with composing for the children and helps the teacher construct consistent, composer-centered goals that enable children to use what they've gained from one situation in many others. In this approach to nonfiction composing and assessment, student response becomes the most central element, not just teacher plans, although the teacher is responding and planning all the time.

In the End

It is important for the teacher to understand that the development of nonfiction composing is a synthetic process in which children are continually putting together different elements of their individual development, their experience of the world and personal relationships, and the composing tools they are acquiring.

Table 6.6. A Teacher Assessment

Record one way in which the children learned to use nonfiction or non-narrative text that they can also use in the next project or situation, or that draws on the children's previous composing.

_____

_____

_____

_____

Record a sequence of experiences in which nonfiction reading or composing is necessary for a purpose the *children* have devised.

_____

_____

_____

_____

Record one composing activity that could lend itself to several different nonfiction/non-narrative composing choices.

_____

_____

_____

_____

Record at least two different ways in which you have used questioning to expand a composing choice (oral, drawn, and/or written).

_____

_____

_____

_____

Record ways in which the composing activity fulfills two child goals.

_____

_____

_____

_____

Record ways in which the composing activity fulfills two teacher goals.

_____

_____

In this way, composing emerges as a true expression of the child's inner world as it is played out in actual situations.

Composing follows processes of development that teachers can neither directly steer nor completely assess, so deeply do they engage the self, even though they surface in moment-to-moment encounters. These are processes that teachers must watch closely in order to follow and thus promote their growth in moments both found and created. At times, we may be truly disappointed that the children do not more fully use the tools we have so carefully offered to the end we've envisaged. At times, we may think we've completely missed the mark. The problem is often that we do not understand. Quite frequently, and usually unexpectedly, children serve us up a Zen koan, a seemingly unanswerable conundrum. That's the joy of this approach to nonfiction composing. Becoming comfortable with the koans—even inviting them—keeps us energized and averts the day when we find ourselves deadeningly sure that there are no surprises left.

References

American Association for the Advancement of Science. (1990). *Science for all Americans*. New York: Oxford University Press.

Bakhtin, M. M. (1981). *The dialogic imagination*. Austin: University of Texas Press.

Banfield, A. (1982). *Unspeakable sentences: Narration and representation in the language of fiction*. Boston: Routledge & Kegan Paul.

Benedict, H. (1999). Fiction vs. nonfiction: Wherein lies the truth? *Poets and Writers, 27*, 46–49.

Berger, K. S. (1986). *The developing person through childhood and adolescence* (2nd ed.). New York: Worth Publishers, Inc.

Berne, S. (2001). Family in the age of anxiety: An interview with Suzanne Berne. *Poets and Writers, 29* (4), 32–37.

Bissex, G. L. (1980). *Gnys at work: A child learns to write and read.* Cambridge, MA: Harvard University Press.

Bloom, H. (2000). *How to read and why*. New York: Scribner.

Board of Education of the City of New York. (1997). *New standards performance standards for English language arts* (New York City edition). Retrieved from http://www.nycenet.edu/ teachers/standards/NYCELAv2.pdf

Bredekamp, S. & Copple, C. (Eds.). (1997). *Developmentally appropriate practice in early childhood programs* (revised edition). Washington, DC: National Association for the Education of Young Children.

Britsch, S. (1988). *The role of spontaneous literacy events in the social lives of three-year-olds*. Paper presented at "A New Look at Language Arts in Early Childhood Education Conference," Berkeley, Calif.

Britsch, S. J. (1992). The development of "story" within the culture of the preschool. *Dissertation Abstracts International, 54* (6), 2045A–2046A.

Britsch, S. J. (2001a). Emergent environmental literacy in the non-narrative compositions of kindergarten children. *Early Childhood Education Journal, 28* (3), 153–159.

Britsch, S. J. (2001b). Assessment for emergent science literacy in classrooms for young children. In D. Shepardson (Ed.),

Assessment in science: A guide to professional development and classroom practice (pp. 101–117). Dordrecht, the Netherlands: Kluwer Academic Publishers.

Bruner, J. (1986). *Actual minds, possible worlds.* Cambridge: Harvard University Press.

Bruner, J. (1988). Research currents: Life as narrative. *Language Arts, 65,* 574–583.

Bruner, J. (1991). The narrative construction of reality. *Critical Inquiry, 18,* 1–21.

Burroway, J. (1996). *Writing fiction* (4th ed.). New York: Harper Collins College Publishers.

Carvajal, D. (1999, October 5). Editor of the Reagan book overcame qualms. *The New York Times,* pp. A1, A19.

Clay, M. M. (1975). *What did I write? Beginning writing behaviour.* Auckland, New Zealand: Heinemann Educational Books.

Collins, J. L. (1998). Strategies for struggling writers. New York: Guilfor Press.

Cooper, P. (1993). *When stories come to school: Telling, writing & performing stories in the early childhood classroom.* New York: Teachers and Writers Collaborative.

Cope, B. & Kalantzis, M. (1993). Introduction: How a genre approach to literacy can transform the way writing is taught. In B. Cope & M. Kalantzis (Eds.), *The powers of literacy: A genre approach to teaching writing* (pp. 1–21). Pittsburgh: University of Pittsburgh Press.

Decker, R. E. & Schwegler, R. A. (1992). *Patterns of exposition.* New York: HarperCollins.

Derewianka, B. (1990). *Exploring how texts work.* Rozelle, New South Wales, Australia: Primary English Teaching Association.

Dietsch, B.M. (2000). *Reasoning and writing well: A rhetoric, research guide, reader and handbook* (2nd ed.). Mountain View, CA: Mayfield Publishing Company.

Donovan, C. A. (2001). Children's development and control of written story and informational genres: Insights from one elementary school. *Research in the Teaching of English, 35* (3), 394–447.

Duckworth, E. (1964). Piaget rediscovered. In R. E. Ripple & V. N. Rockcastle (Eds.), *Piaget rediscovered.* (A report of the Conference on Cognitive Studies and Cornell University Curriculum Development.) Washington, DC: Department of Health, Education and Welfare, Office of Child Development.

Dyson, A. H. (1986). The imaginary worlds of childhood: A multimedia presentation. *Language Arts, 63* (8), 799–808.

Dyson, A. H. (1988). Negotiating among multiple worlds: The space/time dimensions of young children's composing. Technical report no. 15, National Center for the Study of Writing. Berkeley: University of California, Berkeley.

Dyson, A. H. (1989). *Multiple worlds of child writers: Friends learning to write.* New York: Teachers College Press.

Dyson, A. H. (1990). The word and the world: Reconceptualizing written language development or do rainbows mean a lot to little girls? Technical report no. 42, National Center for the Study of Writing. Berkeley: University of California, Berkeley.

Elkind, D. (1987). Early education on its own terms. In S. L. Kagan & E. F. Zigler (Eds.), *Early schooling: The national debate* (pp. 98–115). New Haven, CT: Yale University Press.

Ellis, D. (2000). *Literary lives: Biography and the search for understanding.* New York: Routledge.

Flower, L. (1990). Negotiating academic discourse. In L. Flower, V. Stein, J. Ackerman, M. J. Kantz, K. McCormick, & W. C. Peck (Eds.), *Reading-to-write: Exploring a cognitive and social press* (pp. 221–252). New York: Oxford University Press.

Fox, M. (1993). *Radical reflections: Passionate opinions on teaching, learning, and living.* San Diego: Harcourt, Brace & Company.

Freedman, D., Pisani, R. & Purves, R. (1978). *Statistics.* New York: W. W. Norton.

Gee, J. P. (1987). What is literacy? *Teaching and Learning: The Journal of Natural Inquiry, 2* (1), 3–11.

Genishi, C. & Dyson, A. H. (1984). *Language assessment in the early years.* Norwood, NJ: Ablex.

Gergen, K. J. (1999). *An invitation to social construction.* London: Sage Publications.

Goleman, D., Kaufman, P. & Ray, M. (1992). *The creative spirit.* New York: Penguin Books.

Green, P. (1992). *A matter of fact: Using factual texts in the classroom.* Armadale, Victoria, Australia: Eleanor Curtain Publishing.

Greene, M. (2001). The slow fuse of the possible. *Teachers and Writers, 32* (5), 1–2.

Greenwald, E. A., Persky, H. R., Campbell, J. R., & Mazzeo, J. (1999). *NAEP 1998 writing report card for the nation and the states.* Washington, DC: U.S. Department of Education.

Harlan, W. (1992). *The teaching of science*. London: David Fulton Publishers.

Harvey, S. (1998). *Nonfiction matters: Reading, writing and research in grades 3–8*. York, Maine: Stenhouse.

Hohmann, M., Banet, B., & Weikart, D.P. (1979). *Young children in action*. Ypsilanti, MI: The High/Scope Press.

Holquist, M. (1990). *Dialogism: Bakhtin and his world*. London: Routledge.

Hough, R. A., Nurss, J. R. & Wood, D. (1987). Tell me a story: Making opportunities for elaborated language in early childhood classrooms. *Young Children, 42*, 6–12.

Humphryes, J. (2000). Exploring nature with children. *Young Children, 55* (3), pp. 16–20.

Jones, E. (1986). *Teaching adults: An active learning approach*. Washington, DC: National Association for the Education of Young Children.

Kamberelis, G. (1999). Genre development and learning: Children writing stories, science reports, and poems. *Research in the Teaching of English, 33* (4), 403–460.

Kantz, M. (1987). *Composing from textual sources: Rhetorical stances for writing synthese*. Unpublished doctorial dissertation, Carnegie Mellon University, Pittsburgh.

Kress, G. (1993). Genre as social process. In B. Cope & M. Kalantzis (Eds.), *The powers of literacy: A genre approach to teaching writing* (pp. 22–37). Pittsburgh: University of Pittsburgh Press.

Kress, G. (1994). *Learning to write* (2nd ed.). London: Routledge.

Kress, G. (1999). Genre and the changing contexts for English language arts. *Language Arts, 76* (6), 461–469.

Lightman, A. (2000). *Great ideas in physics*. New York: McGraw-Hill.

Martin, J. R. (1993). Literacy in science: Learning to handle text as technology. In M.A.K. Halliday & J. R. Martin (Eds.), *Writing science: Literacy and discursive power* (pp. 166–202). London: The Falmer Press.

Moffett, J. (1968). *Teaching the universe of discourse*. Boston: Houghton Mifflin Company.

Moline, S. (1995). *I see what you mean: Children at work with visual information*. York, ME: Stenhouse Publishers.

Morrow, L. M. (1997) *Literacy development in the early years: Helping children read and write*. (3rd ed). Needham Heights, MA: Allyn & Bacon.

Moss, B., Leone, S., & Dipillo, M. L. (1997). Exploring the literature of fact: Linking reading and writing through information trade books. *Language Arts, 74* (6), 418–429.

Neuman, S. B., Copple, C., & Bredekamp, S. (2000). *Learning to read and write: Developmentally appropriate practices for young children.* Washington, DC: National Association for the Education of Young Children.

Newkirk, T. (1985). The hedgehog or the fox: The dilemma of writing development. *Language Arts, 62* (6), 593–603.

Newkirk, T. (1987). The non-narrative writing of young children. *Research in the Teaching of English, 21* (1), 121–144.

Newkirk, T. (1989). *More than stories: The range of children's writing.* Portsmouth, NH: Heinemann.

Newkirk, T. (September 13, 2000). A mania for rubrics. *Education Week, 20* (2), 41.

Ochs, E., Taylor, C., Rudolph, D., & Smith, R. (1992). Storytelling as a theory-building activity. *Discourse Processes, 15,* 37–72.

Overbye, D. (2000). *Einstein in love: A scientific romance.* New York: Viking.

Owens, C. (1999). Caught between a rock and a hard place: A natural scientist writes. *Language Arts, 76* (3), 234–240.

Owocki, G. (1999). *Literacy through play.* Portsmouth, NH: Heinemann.

Paley, V. G. (1981). *Wally's stories.* Cambridge: Harvard University Press.

Pappas, C. C. & Pettegrew, B. S. (1998). The role of genre in the psycholinguistic guessing game of reading. *Language Arts, 75* (1), 36–44.

Peters, B. (1997). Genre, antigenre and reinventing the forms of conceptualization. In W. Bishop & H. Ostrom (Eds.), *Genre and writing: Issues, arguments, alternatives* (pp. 199–214). Portsmouth, NH: Heinemann.

Petoskey Regional Chamber of Commerce. (2002). *Petoskey stones.* Retrieved from www.petoskey.com/pstone.html.

Poe, E. A. (1999). The pit and the pendulum. In E. A. Poe, *The complete tales of Edgar Allan Poe.* (pp. 342–353). New York: Barnes and Noble Books.

Rogoff, B. (1990). *Apprenticeship in thinking: Cognitive development in social context.* New York: Oxford University Press.

Romano, T. (2000). *Blending genre, altering style: Writing multigenre papers.* Portsmouth, NH: Heinemann.

Rood, R. N. (1960). *The how and why wonder book of insects.* New York: Grosset & Dunlap.

Rosenblatt, L.M. (1988). Writing and reading: The transactional theory. Technical report no. 13, Center for the Study of Writing. Berkeley: University of California, Berkeley.

Rowe, D. W. (1994). *Preschoolers as authors: Literacy learning in the social world of the classroom.* Cresskill, NJ: Hampton Press.

Schickendanz, J. A. (1999). *Much more than the ABCs: The early stages of reading and writing.* Washington, DC: National Association for the Education of Young Children.

Schroeder, E. J. (1998). As truthful as possible: An interview with Maxine Hong Kingston. In P. Skenazy & T. Martin (Eds.), *Conversations with Maxine Hong Kingston* (pp. 215–228). Jackson: University Press of Mississippi.

Seshachari, N. C. (1998). Reinventing peace: Conversations with tripmaster Maxine Hong Kingston. In P. Skenazy & T. Martin, T. (Eds.), *Conversations with Maxine Hong Kingston* (pp. 192–214). Jackson: University Press of Mississippi.

Shepardson, D. P. & Britsch, S. J. (1997). Children's science journals: Tools for teaching, learning and assessment. *Science and Children, 34,* 13–17, 46–47.

Shepardson, D. P. & Britsch, S. J. (2000). Analyzing children's science journals: What can students' science journals tell us about what they are learning? *Science and Children, 38* (3), 29–33.

Shepardson, D. P. & Britsch, S. J. (2001). The role of children's journals in elementary school science activities. *Journal of Research in Science Teaching, 38* (1), 43–69.

Skenazy, P. (1998). Kingston at the university. In P. Skenazy & T. Martin, T. (Eds.), *Conversations with Maxine Hong Kingston* (pp. 118–158). Jackson: University Press of Mississippi.

Smith, D. B. (1973). *A taste of blackberries.* New York: HarperCollins Publishers.

Tallmadge, J. (2000). A matter of scale: Searching for wildness in the city. In C. McEwen & M. Statman (Eds.). *The alphabet of the trees: A guide to nature writing* (pp. 60–65). New York: Teachers and Writers Collaborative.

Toolan, M. (1988). *Narrative: A critical linguistic introduction.* New York: Routledge.

Tyler, R. W. (1949). *Basic principles of curriculum and instruction.* Chicago: University of Chicago Press.

Vaughn, T. A. (1978). *Mammalogy* (2nd ed.). Philadelphia, PA: W. B. Saunders Company.

Vygotsky, L. S. (1978). *Mind in society: The development of higher psychological processes*. Cambridge: Harvard University Press.

Waters, J., Frantz, J. F., Rottmayer, S., Trickett, M. & Genishi, C. (1992). Learning to see the learning of preschool children. In C. Genishi (Ed.), *Ways of assessing children and curriculum: Stories of early childhood education* (pp. 25–57). New York: Teachers College Press.

Weathers, W. (1980). *An alternate style: Options in composition*. Rochelle Park, NJ: Hayden Book Co.

Werner, H. (1948). *Comparative psychology of mental development*. New York: International Universities Press.

Whitin, D. J. & Whitin, P. (1998). Learning is born of doubting: Cultivating a skeptical stance. *Language Arts, 76* (2), 123–129.

Wignell, P., Martin, J. R. & Eggins, S. (1993). The discourse of geography: Ordering and explaining the experiential world. In M.A.K. Halliday & J. R. Martin (Eds.), *Writing science: Literacy and discursive power* (pp. 136–165). London: The Falmer Press.

Wiley, M. (2000). The popularity of formulaic writing (and why we need to resist). *English Journal, 90* (1), 61–67.

Winterowd, W. R. & Blum, J. (1994). *A teacher's introduction to composition in the rhetorical tradition*. Urbana, IL: National Council of Teachers of English.

Zecker, L. B. (1999). Different texts, different emergent writing forms. *Language Arts, 76*, 483–490.

Index

activity description, 47, 49–55,
    97–98, 110, 124–126,
    136–137, 143
antigenre, 41
argument, 48, 65–66
assessment
    defined, 129–131
    developmental, 132–139
    of genre knowledge, 8,
        35–39, 129–131, 140–141
    logs, 141
    observational, 38, 132–134
    of teachers, 141–145
    standards in, 131–132,
        139–140

Bakhtin, Mikhail M., 2
Banet, Bernard, 142–143
Banfield, Ann, 119
Benedict, Helen, 6, 17, 43
Berger, Kathleen S., 109
Berne, Suzanne, 65
biography, 68–69, 106, 114
Bissex, Glenda, 37
Bloom, Harold, 107
Blum, Jack, 16
Bredekamp, Sue, 98
Britsch, Susan J., 2, 9–11, 12,
    13, 15, 16, 23, 53, 59–60, 63,
    71–73, 76, 90, 113
Bruner, Jerome, 43, 60, 67
Burroway, Janet, 107

Carvajal, Doreen, 120

classification 8, 44, 47, 62–65,
    81–84, 90–91, 94–95, 97, 98,
    99, 106, 110, 113, 114, 118,
    133, 134, 143
Clay, Marie M., 25
Collins, James, 43
composing
    described, xi–xii, 1–4, 9, 25,
        41–42, 101–102
    gestural beginnings of,
        21–23, 25
    in play, 21–31
    questioning in composing,
        96–100
    social gesture of, 23–28,
        31–35, 37, 41–42
    and reading, 121–125
composing choices
    activity description, 47,
        49–55, 97, 138
    argument, 48, 65–66
    classification, 47, 62–65,
        81–84, 88, 90–91, 97, 110
    collection of, 46–49
    concept list, 47, 49–50, 83–84,
        97–98
    how explanation, 47, 59–61, 88,
        92–93, 97–99, 110, 133–139
    letters, 91–93
    narrative reporting, 76–77
    nonfiction narrative, 48,
        66–69, 80, 97
    object description, 47, 49–55,
        97, 110